Application Architecture for .NET:
Designing Applications and Services

ISBN 0-7356-1837-2

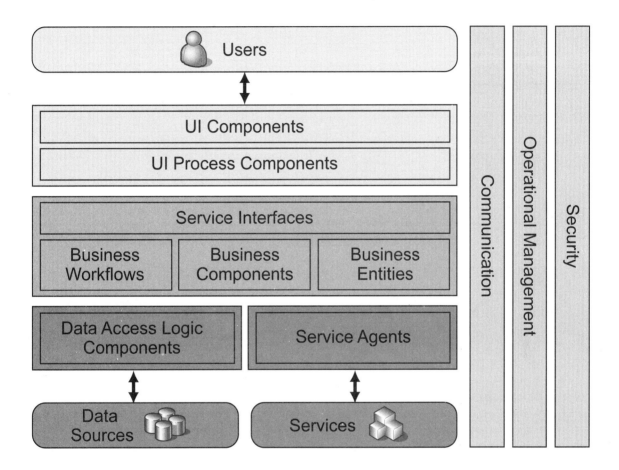

Contents

Chapter 4

Physical Deployment and Operational Requirements   119

Appendixes   151

Feedback and Support   157

Additional Resources   159

1

Introduction

Application Architecture for .NET: Designing Applications and Services provides architecture- and design-level guidance for application architects and developers who need to build distributed solutions with the Microsoft® .NET Framework.

This guide is for you if you:

- Design the high-level architecture for applications or services.
- Recommend appropriate technologies and products for specific aspects of your application or service.
- Make design decisions to meet functional and nonfunctional (operational) requirements.
- Choose appropriate communications mechanisms for your application or service.

This guide identifies the key design decisions you need to make during the early phases of development and provides design-level guidance to help you choose between design options. It helps you develop an overall design by presenting a consistent architecture built of different types of components that will help you achieve a good design and take advantage of the Microsoft platform. Although this guide is not intended to provide implementation-level guidance for each aspect of the application, it does provide references to specific Microsoft Patterns & Practices guides, MSDN articles, and community sites that discuss in detail the various aspects of distributed application design. You can think of this guide as a roadmap of the most important distributed application design issues you will encounter when using the Microsoft platform.

This guide focuses on distributed applications and Web services that may need to provide integration capabilities for multiple data sources and services, and that may require a user interface for one or multiple devices.

The discussion assumes that you are familiar with .NET component development and the basic principles of a layered distributed application design.

Contents Roadmap

This guide consists of five chapters:

- Chapter 1, "Introduction" – Explains how applications and services interrelate.
- Chapter 2, "Designing the Components of an Application or Service" – Walks through the architecture, discussing the roles and design criteria of each component layer.
- Chapter 3, "Security, Operational Management, and Communications Policies" – Details design issues that pertain to the whole application, such as exception management and authorization.
- Chapter 4, "Physical Deployment and Operational Requirements" – Explains how the application design affects deployment and change management, and discusses common deployment patterns used in well-built solutions.
- Appendixes – Contains reference figures and a glossary of terms used in the guide.

These chapters are most valuable when they are read in sequential order, but each chapter provides information that can be useful independent of the other chapters.

Chapter Contents

This chapter contains the following sections:

- Goals of Distributed Application Design
- Services and Service Integration
- Components and Tiers in Applications and Services
- A Sample Scenario

Goals of Distributed Application Design

Designing a distributed application involves making decisions about its logical and physical architecture and the technologies and infrastructure used to implement its functionality. To make these decisions effectively, you must have a sound understanding of the business processes that the application will perform (its functional requirements), and the levels of scalability, availability, security, and maintainability required (its nonfunctional, or operational, requirements).

Your goal is to design an application that:

- Solves the business problem it is designed to address.
- Addresses security considerations from the start, taking into consideration the appropriate authentication mechanisms, authorization logic, and secure communication.

- Provides high performance and is optimized for common operations across deployment patterns.
- Is available and resilient, and can be deployed in redundant, high-availability data centers.
- Scales to meet the expected demands, and supports a large number of activities and users with minimal use of resources.
- Is manageable, allowing operators to deploy, monitor, and troubleshoot the application as appropriate for the scenario.
- Is maintainable. Each piece of functionality should have a predictable location and design taking into account diverse application sizes, teams with varying skill sets, and changing business and technical requirements.
- Works in various application scenarios and deployment patterns.

The design guidance provided in subsequent chapters addresses each of these goals and discusses the reasons for particular design decisions whenever it is important to understand their background.

Services and Service Integration

As the Internet and its related technologies grow, and organizations seek to integrate their systems across departmental and organizational boundaries, a services-based approach to building solutions has evolved. From the consumer's perspective, services are conceptually similar to traditional components, except that services encapsulate their own data and are not strictly speaking part of your application; rather they are used by your application. Applications and services that need to be integrated may be built on different platforms, by different teams, on different schedules, and may be maintained and updated independently. Therefore, it is critical that you implement communication between them with the least coupling possible.

It is recommended that you implement communication between services by using message-based techniques to provide high levels of robustness and scalability. You can implement message communication explicitly (for example, by writing code to send and receive Message Queuing messages), or you can use infrastructure components that manage the communication for you implicitly (for example, by using a Web service proxy generated by Microsoft Visual Studio® .NET).

Note: The term *service* is used in this guide to indicate any external software component that provides business services. This includes, but is not limited to, XML Web services.

Services expose a *service interface* to which all inbound messages are sent. The definition of the set of messages that must be exchanged with a service in order for the service to perform a specific business task constitutes a *contract*. You can think of a service interface as a façade that exposes the business logic implemented in the service to potential consumers.

For example, consider a retail application through which customers order products. The application uses an external credit card authorization service to validate the customer's credit card details and authorize the sale. After the credit card details are verified, a courier service is used to arrange delivery of the goods. The following sequence diagram (Figure 1.1) illustrates this scenario.

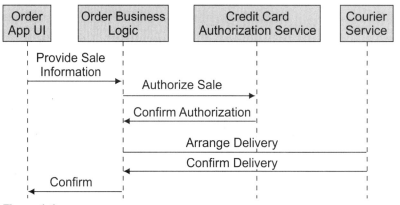

Figure 1.1
A business process that is implemented using services

In this scenario, the credit card authorization service and the courier service each play a role in the overall business process of making a purchase. Unlike ordinary components, services exist in their own trust boundary and manage their own data, outside the application. Therefore you must be sure to establish a secure, authenticated connection between the calling application and the service when using a services-based approach to application development. Additionally, you could implement communication by using a message-based approach, making the design more suitable for describing business processes (sometimes referred to as *business transactions* or *long-running transactions*) and for loose coupling of systems that are common in large, distributed solutions—particularly if the business process involves multiple organizations and diverse platforms.

For example, if message-based communications are used in the process shown in Figure 1.1, the user may receive the order confirmation seconds or hours after the sale information was provided, depending on how responsive the authorization and delivery services are. Message-based communication can also make the design of your business logic independent of the underlying transport protocol used between services.

If your application uses an external service, the internal implementation of the service is irrelevant to your design—as long as the service does what it is supposed to do. You simply need to know the business functionality that the service provides and the details of the contract you must adhere to in order to communicate with it (such as communication format, data schema, authentication mechanism, and so on). In the retail application example, the credit card authorization service provides an interface through which sale and credit card details can be passed to the service, and a response indicating whether or not the sale is approved. From the retail application designer's perspective, what happens inside the credit card authorization service does not matter; the only concern is to determine what data needs to be sent to the service, what responses will be received from the service, and how to communicate with the service.

Internally, services contain many of the same kinds of components that traditional applications do. (The rest of this guide focuses on the various components and their role in the application design.) Services contain logic components that orchestrate the business tasks they perform, business components that implement the actual business logic of the service, and data access components that access the service's data store. In addition, services expose their functionality through service interfaces, which handle the semantics of exposing the underlying business logic. Your application will also call other services through *service agents*, which communicate with the service on behalf of the calling client application.

Although message-based services can be designed to be called synchronously, it can be advantageous to build asynchronous service interfaces, which allow a more loosely coupled approach to distributed application development. The loose coupling that asynchronous communication provides makes it possible to build highly available, scalable, and long-lasting solutions composed of existing services. However, an asynchronous design doesn't provide these benefits for free: Using asynchronous communication means your design may need to take into account such special considerations as message correlation, optimistic data concurrency management, business process compensation, and external service unavailability.

Note: Chapter 3, "Security, Operational Management, and Communications Policies," discusses in detail the issues involved in implementing service communication.

For more information about services and related concepts, see "Application Conceptual View" on MSDN (*http://msdn.microsoft.com/library/en-us/dnea/html/eaappconland.asp*).

Components and Tiers in Applications and Services

It has become a fairly widely accepted tenet of distributed application design that you should divide your application into components providing presentation, business, and data services. Components that perform similar types of functions can be grouped into layers, which in many cases are organized in a stacked fashion so that components "above" a certain layer use the services provided by it, and a given component will use the functionality provided by other components in its own layer and other layers "below" to perform its work.

Note: This guide uses the term *layer* to refer to a component type and uses the term *tier* to refer to physical distribution patterns.

This partitioned view of an application can also be applied to services. From a high-level view, a service-based solution can be seen as being composed of multiple services, each communicating with the others by passing messages. Conceptually, the services can be seen as components of the overall solution. However, internally each service is made up of software components, just like any other application, and these components can be logically grouped into presentation, business, and data services, as shown in Figure 1.2.

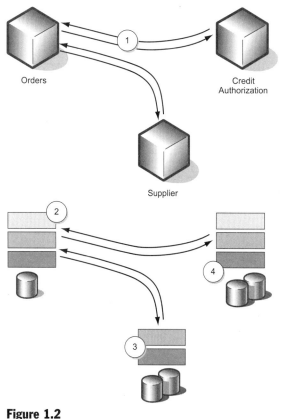

Figure 1.2
A service-based solution

The important points to note about this figure are as follows:

1. Services are usually designed to communicate with each other with the least coupling possible. Using message-based communication helps to decouple the availability and scalability of the services, and relying on industry standards such as XML Web services allows integration with other platforms and technologies.

2. Each service consists of an application with its own data sources, business logic, and user interfaces. A service may have the same internal design as a traditional three-tier application, for example, services (2) and (4) in the previous figure.

3. You can choose to build and expose a service that has no user interface directly associated with it (a service that is designed to be invoked by other applications through a programmatic interface). This is shown in service (3). Notice that the components that make up a service and the components that make up the business layers of an application can be designed in a similar way.

4. Each service encapsulates its own data and manages atomic transactions with its own data sources.

It is important to note that the layers are merely logical groupings of the software components that make up the application or service. They help to differentiate between the different kinds of tasks performed by the components, making it easier to design reusability into the solution. Each logical layer contains a number of discrete component types grouped into sublayers, with each sublayer performing a specific kind of task. By identifying the generic *kinds* of components that exist in most solutions, you can construct a meaningful map of an application or service, and then use this map as a blueprint for your design.

Figure 1.3 shows a simplified view of one application and its layers.

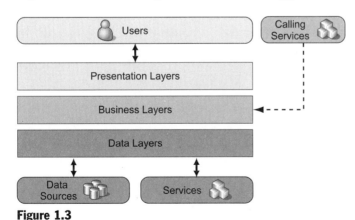

Figure 1.3
Components separated into layers according to their roles

A distributed solution may need to span multiple organizations or physical tiers, in which case it will have its own policies regarding application security, operational management, and communications. These units of trust, or *zones*, can be a physical tier, a data center, or a department, division, or company that has such policies defined. Together, these policies define rules for the environment in which the application is deployed and how services and application tiers communicate. The policies span the entire application, and the way they are implemented affects design decisions at each tier. They also have an impact on each other (for example, the security policy may determine some of the rules in the communication policy, and vice versa).

Note: For more information about security, operational management, and communications policy design, see Chapter 3, "Security, Operational Management, and Communications Policies."

A Sample Scenario

To help identify common kinds of components, this guide describes a sample application that uses external services. Although this guide focuses on a specific example, the design recommendations given apply to most distributed applications, regardless of the actual business scenario.

The sample scenario described in this guide is an extension of the retail application described earlier in this chapter. In this scenario, a retail company offers its customers the choice of ordering products through an e-commerce Web site or by telephone. Internet users can visit the company's Web site and select products from an online catalog. Alternatively, customers can order products from a mail order catalog by telephoning a sales representative, who enters the order details through a Microsoft Windows–based application. After an order is complete, the customer's credit card details are authorized using an external credit card authorization service, and delivery is arranged using an external courier service.

The proposed solution for this scenario is a component-based design that consists of a number of components, as shown in Figure 1.4.

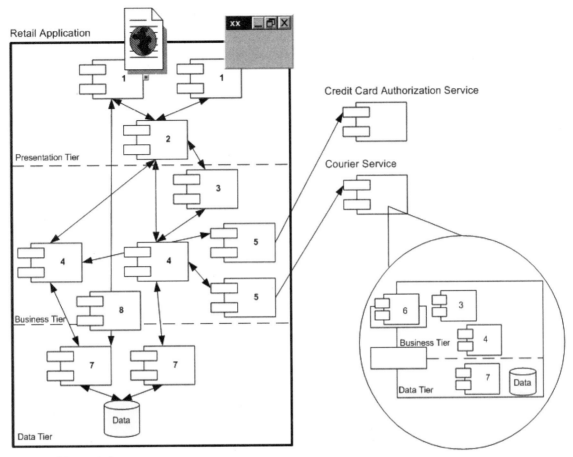

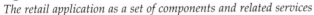

Figure 1.4
The retail application as a set of components and related services

Figure 1.4 shows the retail application as composed of multiple software components, which are grouped into logical tiers according to the kind of functionality they provide. Note that from the standpoint of the retail application, the credit card authorization and courier services can be thought of as external components. However, internally the services are implemented much as ordinary applications are, and contain the same kinds of components (although the services in this scenario do not contain a presentation tier, but publish their functionality through a programmatic service interface).

What's Next?

This chapter has introduced you to service based solutions and has explained how a service, like any other application, is composed of multiple software components that can be grouped into logical tiers. The components that make up an application or service can be described in generic terms. An understanding of the different component types that are commonly used in distributed applications will help you design better solutions.

Chapter 2, "Designing the Components of an Application or Service," describes common component types and provides recommendations on how best to design them.

Designing the Components of an Application or Service

Chapter 1 described how an application or service is composed of multiple components, each performing a different kind of task. Every software solution contains similar kinds of components, regardless of the specific business need it addresses. For example, most applications contain components that access data, encapsulate business rules, handle user interaction, and so on. Identifying the kinds of components commonly found in distributed software solutions will help you build a blueprint for an application or service design.

Chapter Contents

This chapter contains the following sections:

- Component Types
- General Design Recommendations for Applications and Services
- Designing Presentation Layers
- Designing Business Layers
- Designing Data Layers

Component Types

An examination of most business solutions based on a layered component model reveals several common component types. Figure 2.1 shows these component types in one comprehensive illustration.

Note: The term *component* is used in the sense of a piece or part of the overall solution. This includes compiled software components, such as Microsoft .NET assemblies, and other software artifacts such as Web pages and Microsoft® BizTalk® Server Orchestration schedules.

Although the list of component types shown in Figure 2.1 is not exhaustive, it represents the common kinds of software components found in most distributed solutions. These component types are described in depth throughout the remainder of this chapter.

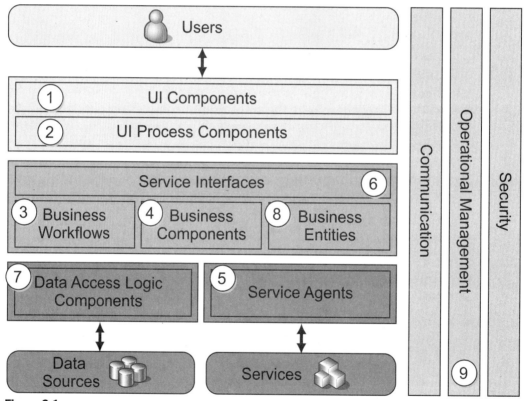

Figure 2.1
Component types in the retail sample scenario

The component types identified in the sample scenario design are:

1. **User interface (UI) components**. Most solutions need to provide a way for users to interact with the application. In the retail application example, a Web site lets customers view products and submit orders, and an application based on the Microsoft Windows® operating system lets sales representatives enter order data for customers who have telephoned the company. User interfaces are implemented using Windows Forms, Microsoft ASP.NET pages, controls, or any other technology you use to render and format data for users and to acquire and validate data coming in from them.

2. **User process components**. In many cases, a user interaction with the system follows a predictable process. For example, in the retail application you could implement a procedure for viewing product data that has the user select a category from a list of available product categories and then select an individual product in the chosen category to view its details. Similarly, when the user makes a purchase, the interaction follows a predictable process of gathering data from the user, in which the user first supplies details of the products to be purchased, then provides payment details, and then enters delivery details. To help synchronize and orchestrate these user interactions, it can be useful to drive the process using separate user process components. This way the process flow and state management logic is not hard-coded in the user interface elements themselves, and the same basic user interaction "engine" can be reused by multiple user interfaces.

3. **Business workflows**. After the required data is collected by a user process, the data can be used to perform a business process. For example, after the product, payment, and delivery details are submitted to the retail application, the process of taking payment and arranging delivery can begin. Many business processes involve multiple steps that must be performed in the correct order and orchestrated. For example, the retail system would need to calculate the total value of the order, validate the credit card details, process the credit card payment, and arrange delivery of the goods. This process could take an indeterminate amount of time to complete, so the required tasks and the data required to perform them would have to be managed. Business workflows define and coordinate long-running, multi-step business processes, and they can be implemented using business process management tools such as BizTalk Server Orchestration.

4. **Business components**. Regardless of whether a business process consists of a single step or an orchestrated workflow, your application will probably require components that implement business rules and perform business tasks. For example, in the retail application, you would need to implement the functionality that calculates the total price of the goods ordered and adds the appropriate delivery charge. Business components implement the business logic of the application.

5. **Service agents**. When a business component needs to use functionality provided in an external service, you may need to provide some code to manage the semantics of communicating with that particular service. For example, the business components of the retail application described earlier could use a service agent to manage communication with the credit card authorization service, and use a second service agent to handle conversations with the courier service. Service agents isolate the idiosyncrasies of calling diverse services from your application, and can provide additional services, such as basic mapping between the format of the data exposed by the service and the format your application requires.

6. **Service interfaces**. To expose business logic as a service, you must create service interfaces that support the communication contracts (message-based communication, formats, protocols, security, exceptions, and so on) its different consumers require. For example, the credit card authorization service must expose a service interface that describes the functionality offered by the service and the required communication semantics for calling it. Service interfaces are sometimes referred to as *business facades*.

7. **Data access logic components**. Most applications and services will need to access a data store at some point during a business process. For example, the retail application needs to retrieve product data from a database to display product details to the user, and it needs to insert order details into the database when a user places an order. It makes sense to abstract the logic necessary to access data in a separate layer of data access logic components. Doing so centralizes data access functionality and makes it easier to configure and maintain.

8. **Business entity components**: Most applications require data to be passed between components. For example, in the retail application a list of products must be passed from the data access logic components to the user interface components so that the product list can be displayed to the users. The data is used to represent real-world business entities, such as products or orders. The business entities that are used internally in the application are usually data structures, such as DataSets, DataReaders, or Extensible Markup Language (XML) streams, but they can also be implemented using custom object-oriented classes that represent the real-world entities your application has to work with, such as a product or an order.

9. **Components for security, operational management, and communication**: Your application will probably also use components to perform exception management, to authorize users to perform certain tasks, and to communicate with other services and applications. These components are discussed in detail in Chapter 3, "Security, Operational Management, and Communications Policies."

General Design Recommendations for Applications and Services

When designing an application or service, you should consider the following recommendations:

- Identify the kinds of components you will need in your application. Some applications do not require certain components. For example, smaller applications that don't need to integrate with other services may not need business workflows or service agents. Similarly, applications that have only one user interface with a small number of elements may not require user process components.

- Design all components of a particular type to be as consistent as possible, using one design model or a small set of design models. This helps to preserve the predictability and maintainability of the design and implementation for all teams. In some cases, it may be hard to maintain a logical design due to technical environments (for example, if you are developing both ASP.NET- and Windows-based user interfaces); however, you should strive for consistency within each environment. In some cases, you can use a base class for all components that follow a similar pattern, such as data access logic components.

- Understand how components communicate with each other before choosing physical distribution boundaries. Keep coupling low and cohesion high by choosing coarse-grained, rather than chatty, interfaces for remote communication.

- Keep the format used for data exchange consistent within the application or service. If you must mix data representation formats, keep the number of formats low. For example, you may return data in a DataReader from data access logic components to do fast rendering of data in Microsoft ASP.NET, but use DataSets for consumption in business processes. However, be aware that mixing XML strings, DataSets, serialized objects, DataReaders, and other formats in the same application will make the application more difficult to develop, extend, and maintain.

- Keep code that enforces policies (such as security, operational management, and communication restrictions) abstracted as much as possible from the application business logic. Try to rely on attributes, platform application programming interfaces (APIs), or utility components that provide "single line of code" access to functionality related to the policies, such as publishing exceptions, authorizing users, and so on.

- Determine at the outset what kind of layering you want to enforce. In a strict layering system, components in layer A cannot call components in layer C; they always call components in layer B. In a more relaxed layering system, components in a layer can call components in other layers that are not immediately below it. In all cases, try to avoid upstream calls and dependencies, in which layer C invokes layer B. You may choose to implement a relaxed layering to prevent cascading effects throughout all layers whenever a layer close to the bottom changes, or to prevent having components that do nothing but forward calls to layers underneath.

Designing Presentation Layers

The presentation layer contains the components that are required to enable user interaction with the application. The most simple presentation layers contain user interface components, such as Windows Forms or ASP.NET Web Forms. For more complex user interactions, you can design user process components to orchestrate the user interface elements and control the user interaction. User process components are especially useful when the user interaction follows a predictable flow of steps, such as when a wizard is used to accomplish a task. Figure 2.2 shows the component types in the presentation layer.

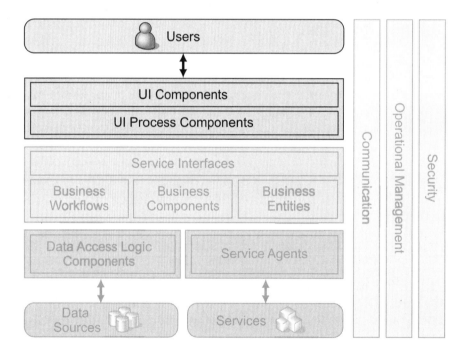

Figure 2.2
Presentation layer

In the case of the retail application, two user interfaces are required: one for the e-commerce Web site that the customers use, and another for the Windows Forms–based applications that the sales representatives use. Both types of users will perform similar tasks through these user interfaces. For example, both user interfaces must provide the ability to view the available products, add products to a shopping basket, and specify payment details as part of a checkout process. This process can be abstracted in a separate user process component to make the application easier to maintain.

Designing User Interface Components

You can implement user interfaces in many ways. For example, the retail application requires a Web-based user interface and a Windows-based user interface. Other kinds of user interfaces include voice rendering, document-based programs, mobile client applications, and so on. User interface components manage interaction with the user. They display data to the user, acquire data from the user, and interpret events that the user raises to act on business data, change the state of the user interface, or help the user progress in his task.

User interfaces usually consist of a number of elements on a page or form that display data and accept user input. For example, a Windows-based application could contain a DataGrid control displaying a list of product categories, and a command button control used to indicate that the user wants to view the products in the selected category. When a user interacts with a user interface element, an event is raised that calls code in a controller function. The controller function, in turn, calls business components, data access logic components, or user process components to implement the desired action and retrieve any necessary data to be displayed. The controller function then updates the user interface elements appropriately. Figure 2.3 shows the design of a user interface.

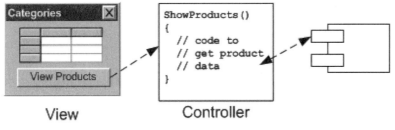

Figure 2.3
User interface design

User Interface Component Functionality

User interface components must display data to users, acquire and validate data from user input, and interpret user gestures that indicate the user wants to perform an operation on the data. Additionally, the user interface should filter the available actions to let users perform only the operations that are appropriate at a certain point in time.

User interface components:

- Do not initiate, participate in, or vote on transactions.
- Have a reference to a current user process component if they need to display its data or act on its state.
- Can encapsulate both view functionality and a controller.

When accepting user input, user interface components:

- Acquire data from users and assist in its entry by providing visual cues (such as tool tips), validation, and the appropriate controls for the task.
- Capture events from the user and call controller functions to tell the user interface components to change the way they display data, either by initiating an action on the current user process, or by changing the data of the current user process.
- Restrict the types of input a user can enter. For example, a **Quantity** field may limit user entries to numerical values.
- Perform data entry validation, for example by restricting the range of values that can be entered in a particular field, or by ensuring that mandatory data is entered.
- Perform simple mapping and transformations of the information provided by the user controls to values needed by the underlying components to do their work (for example, a user interface component may display a product name but pass the product ID to underlying components).
- Interpret user gestures (such as a drag-and-drop operation or button clicks) and call a controller function.
- May use a utility component for caching. In ASP.NET, you can specify caching on the output of a user interface component to avoid re-rendering it every time. If your application contains visual elements representing reference data that changes infrequently and is not used in transactional contexts, and these elements are shared across large numbers of users, you should cache them. You should cache visual elements that are shared across large numbers of users, representing reference data that changes infrequently and that is not used in transactional contexts.

- May use a utility component for paging. It is common, particularly in Web applications, to show long lists of data as paged sets. It is common to have a "helper" component that will keep track of the current page the user is on and thus invoke the data access logic component "paged query" functions with the appropriate values for page size and current page. Paging can occur without interaction of the user process component.

When rendering data, user interface components:

- Acquire and render data from business components or data access logic components in the application.
- Perform formatting of values (such as formatting dates appropriately).
- Perform any localization work on the rendered data (for example, using resource strings to display column headers in a grid in the appropriate language for the user's locale).
- Typically render data that pertains to a business entity. These entities are usually obtained from the user process component, but may also be obtained from the data components. UI components may render data by data-binding their display to the correct attributes and collections of the entity components, if the entity is already available. If you are managing entity data as DataSets, this is very simple to do. If you have implemented custom entity objects, you may need to implement some extra code to facilitate the data binding.
- Provide the user with status information, for example by indicating when an application is working in "disconnected" or "connected" mode.
- May customize the appearance of the application based on user preferences or the kind of client device used.
- May use a utility component to provide undo functionality. Many applications need to let a user undo certain operations. This is usually performed by keeping a fixed-length stack of "old value-new value" data for specific data items or whole entities. When the operation has involved a business process, you should not expose the compensation as a simple undo function, but as an explicit operation.
- May use a utility component to provide clipboard functionality. In many Windows-based applications, it is useful to provide clipboard capabilities for more than just scalar values—for example, you may want to let your users copy and paste a full customer object. Such functionality is usually implemented by placing XML strings in the Clipboard in Windows, or by having a global object that keeps the data in memory if the clipboard is application-specific.

Windows Desktop User Interfaces

Windows user interfaces are used when you have to provide disconnected or offline capabilities or rich user interaction, or even integration with the user interfaces of other applications. Windows user interfaces can take advantage of a wide range of state management and persistence options and can access local processing power. There are three main families of standalone user interfaces: "full-blown" Windows-based applications, Windows-based applications that include embedded HTML, and application plug-ins that can be used within a host application's user interface:

- **"Full-blown" desktop/tablet PC user interfaces built with Windows Forms**

  Building a Windows-based application involves building an application with Windows Forms and controls where your application provides all or most of the data rendering functionality. This gives you a great deal of control over the user experience and total control over the look and feel of the application. However, it ties you to a client platform, and the application needs to be deployed to the users (even if the application is deployed by downloading it over an HTTP connection).

- **Embedded HTML**

  You can choose to implement the entire user interface using Windows Forms, or you can use additional embedded HTML in your Windows-based applications. Embedded HTML allows for greater run-time flexibility (because the HTML may be loaded from external resources or even a database in connected scenarios) and user customization. However, you must carefully consider how to prevent malicious script from being introduced in the HTML, and additional coding is required to load the HTML, display it, and hook up the events from the control with your application functions.

- **Application plug-ins**

  Your use cases may suggest that the user interface of your application could be better implemented as a plug-in for other applications, such as Microsoft Office, AutoCAD, Customer Relationship Management (CRM) solutions, engineering tools, and so on. In this case, you can leverage all of the data acquisition and display logic of the host application and provide only the code to gather the data and work with your business logic.

  Most modern applications support plug-ins as either Component Object Model (COM) or .NET objects supporting a specified interface, or as embedded development environments (such as the Microsoft Visual Basic® development system, which is widely supported in most common Windows-based applications) that can, in turn, invoke custom objects. Some embedded environments (including Visual Basic) even provide a forms engine that enables you add to the user interface experience beyond that provided by the host application. For more information about using Visual Basic in host applications, see "Microsoft Visual

Basic for Applications and Windows DNA 2000" on MSDN (*http:// msdn.microsoft.com/library/default.asp?url=/library/en-us/dndna/html/vba4dna.asp*).

For information about working with .NET from Microsoft Office, see "Microsoft Office and .NET Interoperability" on MSDN (*http://msdn.microsoft.com/library /default.asp?url=/library/en-us/dnofftalk/html/office11012001.asp*).

When creating a Windows Forms-based application, consider the following recommendations:

- Rely on data binding to keep data synchronized across multiple forms that are open simultaneously. This alleviates the need to write complex data synchronization code.

- Try to avoid hard-coding relationships between forms, and rely on the user process component to open them and synchronize data and events. You should be especially careful to avoid hard-coding relationships from child forms to parent forms. For example, a product details window can be reused from other places in the application, not just from an order entry form, so you should avoid implementing functionality in the product details form that links directly to the order entry form. This makes your user interface elements more reusable.

- Implement error handlers in your forms. Doing so prevents the user from seeing an unfriendly .NET exception window and having the application fail if you have not handled exceptions elsewhere. All event handlers and controller functions should include exception catches. Additionally, you may want to create a custom exception class for your user interface that includes metadata to indicate whether the failed operation can be retried or canceled.

- Validate user input in the user interface. Validation should occur at the stages in the user's task or process that allow point-in-time validations (allowing the user to enter some of the required data, continue with a separate task, and return to the current task). In some cases, you should proactively enable and disable controls and visually cue the user when invalid data is entered. Validating user input in the user interface prevents unnecessary round trips to server-side components when invalid data has been entered.

- If you are creating custom user controls, expose only the public properties and methods that you actually need. This makes the components more maintainable.

- Implement your controller functions as separate functions in your Windows Forms or in .NET classes that will be deployed with your client. Do not implement controller functionality directly in control event handlers. Writing controller logic in event handlers reduces the maintainability of the application, because you may need to invoke the same function from other events in the future.

For example, the event handler for a command button named addItem's click event should call a more general procedure to accomplish its task, as shown in the following code.

```
private void addItem_Click(object sender, System.EventArgs e)
{
   AddItemToBasket(selectedProduct, selectedQuantity)
}

public void AddItemToBasket(int ProductID, int Quantity)
{
   // code to add the item to the basket
}
```

Internet Browser User Interfaces

The retail application described in this guide requires a Web-based user interface to allow customers to place orders through the Internet. Web-based user interfaces allow for standards-based user interfaces across many devices and platforms. You develop Web-based user interfaces for .NET-based applications with ASP.NET. ASP.NET provides a rich environment where you can create complex Web-based interfaces with support for important features such as:

- A consistent development environment that is also used for creating the other components of the application.
- User interface data binding.
- Component-based user interfaces with controls.
- Access to the integrated .NET security model.
- Rich caching and state management options.
- Availability, performance, and scalability of Web processing.

When you need to implement an application for a browser, ASP.NET provides the functionality needed to publish a Web page-based user interface. Consider the following design recommendations for ASP.NET user interfaces:

- Implement a custom error page, and a global exception handler in Global.asax. This provides you with a catch-all exception function that prevents the user from seeing unfriendly pages in case of a problem.
- ASP.NET has a rich validation framework that optimizes the task of making sure that data entered by the user conforms to certain criteria. However, the client validation performed at the browser relies on JavaScript being enabled on the client, so you should validate data on your controller functions as well, just in case a user has a browser with no JavaScript support (or with JavaScript disabled). If your user process has a Validate control function, call it before transitioning to other pages to perform point-in-time validation.

- If you are creating Web user controls, expose only the public properties and methods that you actually need. This improves maintainability.

- Use the ASP.NET view state to store page specific state, and keep session and application state for data with a wider scope. This approach makes it easier to maintain and improves scalability.

- Your controller functions should invoke the actions on a user process component to guide the user through the current task rather than redirecting the user to the page directly. The user process component may call the Redirect function to have the server display a different page. To do so, you must reference the System.Web namespace from your user process components. (Note that this means your user process component will not be reusable from Windows-based applications, so you may decide to implement Redirect calls in a different class.)

- Implement your controller functions as separate functions in your ASP.NET pages or in .NET classes that will be deployed with your Web pages. Writing business logic in ASP.NET-provided event handlers reduces the maintainability of the site, because you may need to invoke the same function from other events in the future. Doing so also requires greater skill on the part of developers writing UI-only code.

For example, suppose the retail site Web site contains a page on which a command button can be clicked to add a product to the user's shopping basket. The ASP.NET markup for the control might look like the following line of code.

```
<asp:Button id="addItem" OnClick="addItem_Click"/>
```

As you can see from this code, the button's OnClick event is handled by a function named addItem_Click. However, the event handler should not contain the code to perform the required action (in this case, add an item to the basket), but rather it should call another general function, as shown in the following code.

```
private void addItem_Click(object sender, System.EventArgs e)
{
   AddItemToBasket(selectedProduct, selectedQuantity)
}

public void AddItemToBasket(int ProductID, int Quantity)
{
   // code to add the item to the basket
}
```

This additional layer of abstraction ensures that the code required to perform controller tasks can be reused by multiple user interface elements.

For general information about ASP.NET, see the ASP.NET section of MSDN (*http://msdn.microsoft.com/library/default.asp?url=/nhp/default.asp?contentid=28000440*) and the official ASP.NET site (*http://asp.net*).

In many applications, it is important to provide an extensible framework where multiple panes with different purposes are displayed. In Web-based applications, you also need to provide a home page or root user interface where tasks and information relevant to the user are displayed in a context- and device-sensitive way. Microsoft provides the following resources to help you implement Web-based portals:

- Microsoft Content Management Server (*http://msdn.microsoft.com/library /default.asp?url=/nhp/Default.asp?contentid=28001368*)
- Microsoft SharePoint Portal™ Server 2001 (*http://msdn.microsoft.com/library /default.asp?url=/library/en-us/spssdk/html/_welcome_to_tahoe.asp*)
- IBuySpy Portal (*http://msdn.microsoft.com/library/en-us/dnbda/html /bdasampibsport.asp*)

Mobile Device User Interfaces

Mobile devices such as handheld PCs, Wireless Application Protocol (WAP) phones, and iMode devices are becoming increasingly popular, and building user interfaces for a mobile form factor presents its own unique challenges.

In general, a user interface for a mobile device needs to be able to display information on a much smaller screen than other common applications, and it must offer acceptable usability for the devices being targeted. Because user interaction can be awkward on many mobile devices, particularly mobile phones, you should design your mobile user interfaces with minimal data input requirements. A common strategy is to combine the use of mobile devices with a full-sized Web- or Windows-based application and allow users to preregister data through the desktop-based client, and then select it when using the mobile client. For example, an e-commerce application may allow users to register credit card details through the Web site, so that a preregistered credit card can be selected from a list when orders are placed from a mobile device (thus avoiding the requirement to enter full credit card details using a mobile telephone keypad or personal digital assistant [PDA] stylus).

Web User Interfaces

A wide range of mobile devices support Internet browsing. Some use micro browsers that support a subset of HTML 3.2, some require data to be sent in Wireless Markup Language (WML), and some support other standards such as Compact HTML (cHTML). You can use the Microsoft Mobile Internet Toolkit to create ASP.NET-based Web applications that send the appropriate markup standard to each client based on the device type as identified in the request header. Doing so allows you to create a single Web application that targets a multitude of different mobile clients including Pocket PC, WAP phones, iMode phones, and others.

As with other kinds of user interface, you should try to minimize the possibility of users entering invalid data in a mobile Web page. The Mobile Internet Toolkit includes client-side validation controls such as the CompareValidator, CustomValidator, RegularExpressionValidator, and RequiredFieldValidator controls, which can be used with multiple client device types. You can also use the properties of input fields such as Textbox controls to limit the kind of input accepted (for example by accepting only numeric input). However, you should always allow for client devices that may not support client-side validation, and perform additional checks after the data has been posted to the server.

For more information about the Mobile Internet Toolkit, see the Microsoft Mobile Internet Toolkit page on MSDN (*http://msdn.microsoft.com/vstudio/device /mitdefault.asp*).

Smart Device User Interfaces

The Pocket PC is a feature-rich device based on the Windows CE operating system on which you can develop both disconnected and connected (usually through wireless) user interfaces. The Pocket PC platform includes handheld PDA devices and smart phones, which combine PDA and phone features.

Microsoft provides the .NET Compact Framework for Pocket PC and other Windows CE platforms. The compact framework contains a subset of the full .NET Framework and allows the development of rich .NET–based applications for mobile devices. Developers can use the Smart Device Extensions for Visual Studio .NET to create applications that target the .NET Compact Framework.

As with regular Windows-based user interfaces, you should provide exception handling in your mobile device to inform the user when an operation fails, and allow the user to retry or cancel it as appropriate.

No input validation controls are provided in the Smart Device Extensions for Microsoft Visual Studio® .NET, so you must implement your own client-side validation logic to ensure that all data entry is valid.

For more resources for Pocket PC platform development and the .NET Compact Framework, see the Smart Device Extensions page on MSDN (*http:// msdn.microsoft.com/vstudio/device/smartdev.asp*).

Another mobile form factor for rich clients that you may want to consider is the Tablet PC. Tablet PCs are Windows XP–based portable devices that support user interaction through a "pen and ink" metaphor in which the user "draws" and "writes" on the screen. Since the Tablet PC is based on Windows XP, the full .NET Framework can be leveraged. An additional API for handling "pen and ink" interactions is also available. For more information about designing applications for the Tablet PC, see Design Recommendations for Exploiting the Pocket PC on MSDN (*http://msdn.microsoft.com/library/en-us/tpcsdk10/html/whitepapers/designguide /tbconuxdgformfactorpenandink.asp*).

Document-based User Interfaces

Rather than build a custom Windows-based desktop application to facilitate user interaction, you might find that it makes more sense in some circumstances to allow users to interact with the system through documents created in common productivity tools such as Microsoft Word or Microsoft Excel. Documents are a common metaphor for working with data. In some applications, you may benefit from having users enter or view data in document form in the tools they commonly use. Consider the following document-based solutions:

- **Reporting data**. Your application (Windows- or Web-based) may provide the user with a feature that lets him or her see data in a document of the appropriate type—for example, showing invoice data as a Word document, or a price list as an Excel spreadsheet.

- **Gathering data**. You could let sales representatives enter purchase information for telephone customers in Excel spreadsheets to create a customer order document, and then submit the document to your business process.

There are two common ways to integrate a document experience in your applications, each broken down into two common scenarios: gathering data from users and reporting data to users.

Working with Documents from the Outside

You can work with documents "from the outside," treating them as an entity. In this scenario, your code operates on a document that has no specific awareness of the application. This approach has the advantage that the document file may be preserved beyond a specific session. This model is useful when you have "freeform" areas in the document that your application doesn't need to deal with but you may need to preserve. For example, you can choose this model to allow users to enter information in a document on a mobile device and take advantage of the Pocket PC ActiveSync capabilities to synchronize data between the document on the mobile device and a document kept on the server. In this design model, your user interface will perform the following functions:

- Gathering data. A user can enter information in a document, starting with a blank document, or most typically, starting with a predefined template that has specific fields.

  The user then submits the document to a Windows-based application or uploads it to a Web-based application. The application scans the document's data and fields through the document's object model, and then performs the necessary actions.

  At this point, you may decide either to preserve the document after processing or to dispose of it. Typically, documents are preserved to maintain a tracking history or to save additional data that the user has entered in freeform areas.

- Reporting data. In this case, a Windows- or Web-based user interface provides a way to generate a document that shows some data, such as a sales invoice. The reporting code will usually take data from the ongoing user process, business process, and/or data access logic components and either call macros on the document application to inject the data and format it, or save a document with the correct file format and then return it to the user. You can return the document by saving it to disk and providing a link to it (you would need to save the document in a central store in load-balanced Web farms) or by including it as part of the response.

  When returning documents in Web-based applications, you have to decide whether to display the document in the browser for the user to view, or to present the user with an option to save the document to disk. This is usually controlled by setting the correct MIME type on the response of an ASP.NET page. In Web environments, you need to follow file naming conventions carefully to prevent concurrent users from overwriting each other's files.

Working with Documents from the Inside

When you want to provide an integrated user experience within the document, you can embed the application logic in the document itself. In this design model, your user interface performs the following functions:

- Gathering data. Users can enter data in documents with predefined forms, and then specific macros can be invoked on the template to gather the right data and invoke your business or user process components. This approach provides a more integrated user experience, because the user can just click a custom button or menu option in the host application to perform the work, rather than having to submit the entire document.

- Reporting data. You can implement custom menu entries and buttons in your documents that gather some data from the server and display it. You can also choose to use smart tags in your documents to provide rich inline integration functionality across all Microsoft Office productivity tools. For example, you can provide a smart tag that lets users display full customer contact information from the CRM database whenever a sales representative types in a customer name in the document.

Regardless of whether you work with a document from the inside or from the outside, you should provide validation logic to ensure that all user input is valid. You can achieve this in part by limiting the data types of fields, but in most cases you will need to implement custom functionality to check user input, and display error messages when invalid data is detected. Microsoft Office–based documents can include custom macros to provide this functionality.

For information about how to integrate a purely Office-based UI with your business processes, see "Microsoft Office XP Resource Kit for BizTalk Server Version 2.0" (*http://msdn.microsoft.com/downloads/default.asp?url=/downloads/sample.asp?url=/msdn-files/027/001/743/msdncompositedoc.xml*).

For more information about working with Office and .NET, see MSDN. The following two articles will help you get started with Office and .NET-based application development:

- "Introducing .NET to Office Developers" (*http://msdn.microsoft.com/library/default.asp?url=/library/en-us/dnofftalk/html/office10042001.asp*)

- "Microsoft Office and .NET Interoperability" (*http://msdn.microsoft.com/library/default.asp?url=/library/en-us/dnofftalk/html/office11012001.asp*)

You can manage document-based workflows by taking advantage of the services provided by Microsoft SharePoint Portal™. This product can manage the user process and provides rich metadata and search capabilities.

Accessing Data Access Logic Components from the User Interface

Some applications' user interfaces need to render data that is readily available as queries exposed by data access logic components. Regardless of whether your user interface components invoke data access logic components directly, you should not mix data access logic with business processing logic.

Accessing data access logic components directly from your user interface may seem to contradict the layering concept. However, it is useful in this case to adopt the perspective of your application as one homogenous service—you call it, and it's up to it to decide what internal components are best suited to respond to a request.

You should allow direct data access logic component access to user interface components when:

- You are willing to tightly couple data access methods and schemas with user interface semantics. This coupling requires joint maintenance of user interface changes and schema changes.

- Your physical deployment places data access logic components and user interface components together, allowing you to get data in streaming formats (such as DataReaders) from data access logic components that can be bound directly to the output of ASP.NET user interfaces for performance. If you deploy data access and business process logic on different servers, you cannot take advantage of this capability. From an operational perspective, allowing direct access to the data access logic components to take advantage of streaming capabilities means that you will need to provide access to the database from where the data access logic components are deployed—possibly including access through firewall ports. For more information, see Chapter 4, "Physical Deployment and Operational Requirements."

Designing User Process Components

A user interaction with your application may follow a predictable process; for example, the retail application may require users to enter product details, view the total price, enter payment details, and finally enter delivery address information. This process involves displaying and accepting input from a number of user interface elements, and the state for the process (which products have been ordered, the credit card details, and so on) must be maintained between each transition from one step in the process to another. To help coordinate the user process and handle the state management required when displaying multiple user interface pages or forms, you can create user process components.

Note: Implementing a user interaction with user process components is not a trivial task. Before committing to this approach, you should carefully evaluate whether or not your application requires the level of orchestration and abstraction provided by user process components.

User process components are typically implemented as .NET classes that expose methods that can be called by user interfaces. Each method encapsulates the logic necessary to perform a specific action in the user process. The user interface creates an instance of the user process component and uses it to transition through the steps of the process. The names of the particular forms or ASP.NET pages to be displayed for each step in the process can be hard-coded in the user process component (thus tightly binding it to specific user interface implementations), or they can be retrieved from a metadata store such as a configuration file (making it easier to reuse the user process component from multiple user interface implementations). Designing user process components to be used from multiple user interfaces will result in a more complex implementation in order to isolate device-specific issues, but can help you distribute the user interface development work between multiple teams, each using the same user process component.

User process components coordinate the display of user interface elements. They are abstracted from the data rendering and acquisition functionality provided in the user interface components. You should design them with globalization in mind, to allow for localization to be implemented in the user interface. For example, you should endeavor to use culture-neutral data formats and use Unicode string formats internally to make it easier to consume the user process components from a localized user interface.

The following code shows how a user process component for a checkout process might look.

```
public class PurchaseUserProcess
{
  public PurchaseUserProcess()
  {
```

```
      // create a guid to track this activity
      userActivityID = System.Guid.NewGuid();
   }

   private int customerID;
   private DataSet orderData;
   private DataSet paymentData;
   private Guid userActivityID;
   public bool webUI; // flag to indicate that the client UI is a Web site (or not)

   public void ShowOrder()
   {
     if(webUI)
     {
       //Code to display the Order Details page
       System.Web.HttpContext.Current.Response.Redirect
                        ("http://www.myserver.com/OrderDetails.aspx");
     }
     else // must be a Windows UI
     {
       //code to display the Order Details window.
       OrderDetails = new OrderDetailsForm();
       OrderDetails.Show();
     }
   }
   public void EnterPaymentDetails()
   {
     // code to display the Payment Details page or window goes here
   }
   public void PlaceOrder()
   {
     // code to place the order goes here
     ShowConfirmation();
   }
   public void ShowConfirmation()
   {
     // code to display the confirmation page or window goes here
   }
   public void Finish()
   {
     //code to go back to the main page or window goes here
   }
   public void SaveToDataBase()
   {
     //code to save your order and payment info in the private variables
     //to a database goes here
   }
   public void ResumeCheckout(System.Guid ProcessID)
   {
     // code to reload the process state from the database goes here
   }
   public void Validate()
   {
```

```
    //you would place code here to make sure the process
    //instance variables have the right information for the current step
  }
}
```

Separating the user interaction functionality into user interface and user process components provides the following advantages:

- Long-running user interaction state is more easily persisted, allowing a user interaction to be abandoned and resumed, possibly even using a different user interface. For example, a customer could add some items to a shopping cart using the Web-based user interface, and then call a sales representative later to complete the order.

- The same user process can be reused by multiple user interfaces. For example, in the retail application, the same user process could be used to add a product to a shopping basket from both the Web-based user interface and the Windows Forms-based application.

An unstructured approach to designing user interface logic may result in undesirable situations as the size of the application grows or new requirements are introduced. If you need to add a specific user interface for a given device, you may need to redesign the data flow and control logic.

Partitioning the user interaction flow from the activities of rendering data and gathering data from the user can increase your application's maintainability and provide a clean design to which you can easily add seemingly complex features such as support for offline work. Figure 2.4 shows how the user interface and user process can be abstracted from one another.

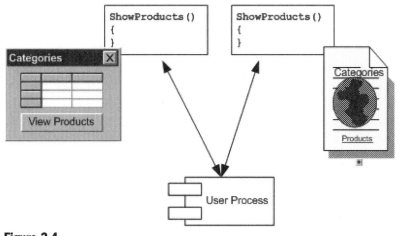

Figure 2.4
User interfaces and user process components

User process components help you to resolve the following user interface design issues:

- **Handling concurrent user activities**. Some applications may allow users to perform multiple tasks at the same time by making more than one user interface element available. For example, a Windows-based application may display multiple forms, or a Web application may open a second browser window.

  User process components simplify the state management of multiple ongoing processes by encapsulating all the state needed for the process in a single component. You can map each user interface element to a particular instance of the user process by incorporating a custom process identifier into your design.

- **Using multiple panes for one activity**. If multiple windows or panes are used in a particular user activity, it is important to keep them synchronized. In a Web application, a user interface usually displays a set of elements in a same page (which may include frames) for a given user activity. However, in rich client applications, you may actually have many non-modal windows affecting just one particular process. For example, you may have a product category selector window floating in your application that lets you specify a particular category, the products in which will be displayed in another window.

  User process components help you to implement this kind of user interface by centralizing the state for all windows in a single location. You can further simplify synchronization across multiple user interface elements by using data bindable formats for state data.

- **Isolating long-running user activities from business-related state**. Some user processes can be paused and resumed later. The intermediate state of the user process should generally be stored separately from the application's business data. For example, a user could specify some of the information required to place an order, and then resume the checkout process at a later time. The pending order data should be persisted separately from the data relating to completed orders, allowing you to perform business operations on completed order data (for example, counting the number of orders placed in the current month) without having to implement complex filtering rules to avoid operating on incomplete orders.

  User activities, just like business processes, may have a "timeout" specified, when the activity has to be cancelled and the right compensatory actions should be taken on the business process.

  You can design your user process components to be serializable, or to store their state separately from the application's business data.

Separating a User Process from the User Interface

To separate a user process from the user interface:

1. Identify the business process or processes that the user interface process will help to accomplish. Identify how the user sees this as a task (you can usually do this by consulting the sequence diagrams that you created as part of your requirements analysis).

2. Identify the data needed by the business processes. The user process will need to be able to submit this data when necessary.

3. Identify additional state you will need to maintain throughout the user activity to assist rendering and data capture in the user interface.

4. Design the visual flow of the user process and the way that each user interface element receives or gives control flow.

You will also need to implement code to map a particular user interface session to the related user process:

- ASP.NET pages will have to obtain the current user process by getting a reference from the Session object, or by rehydrating the process from another storage medium, such as a database. You will need this reference in event handlers for the controls on your Web page.

- Your windows or controls need to keep a reference to the current user process component. You can keep this reference in a member variable. You should not keep it in a global variable, though, because if you do, composing user interfaces will become very complicated as your application user interface grows.

User Process Component Functionality

User process components:

- Provide a simple way to combine user interface elements into user interaction flows without requiring you to redevelop data flow and control logic.

- Separate the conceptual user interaction flow from the implementation or device where it occurs.

- Encapsulate how exceptions may affect the user process flow.

- Keep track of the current state of the user interaction.

- Should not start or participate in transactions. They keep internal data related to application business logic and their internal state, persisting the data as required.

- Maintain internal business-related state, usually holding on to one or more business entities that are affected by the user interaction. You can keep multiple entities in private variables or in an internal array or appropriate collection type. In the case of an ASP.NET-based application, you may also choose to keep references to this data in the Session object, but doing so limits the useful lifetime of the user process.

- May provide a "save and continue later" feature by which a particular user interaction may be restarted in another session. You can implement this functionality by saving the internal state of the user process component in some persistent form and providing the user with a way to continue a particular activity later. You can create a custom task manager utility component to control the current activation state of the process. The user process state can be stored in one of a number of places:

  - If the user process can be continued from other devices or computers, you will need to store it centrally in a location such as a database.

  - If you are running in a disconnected environment, the user process state will need to be stored locally on the user device.

  - If your user interface process is running in a Web farm, you will need to store any required state on a central server location, so that it can be continued from any server in the farm.

- May initialize internal state by calling a business process component or data access logic components.

- Typically will not be implemented as Enterprise Services components. The only reason to do so would be to use the Enterprise Services role-based authorization capabilities.

- Can be started by a custom utility component that manages the menus in your application.

User Process Component Interface Design

The interface of your user process components can expose the following kinds of functionality, as shown in Figure 2.5.

- **User process "actions" (1)**. These are the interface of actions that typically trigger a change in the state of the user process. Actions are implemented in user process component methods, as demonstrated by the ShowOrder, EnterPaymentDetails, PlaceOrder, and Finish methods in the code sample discussed earlier. You should try to encapsulate calls to business components in these action methods (6).

- **State access methods (2)**. You can access the business-specific and business-agnostic state of the user process by using fine-grained get and set properties that expose one value, or by exposing the set of business entities that the user process deals with (5). For example, in the code sample discussed earlier, the user process state can be retrieved through public DataSet properties.

- **State change events (3)**. These events are fired whenever the business-related state or business-agnostic state of the user process changes. Sometimes you will need to implement these change notifications yourself. In other cases, you may be storing your data through a mechanism that already does this intrinsically (for example, a DataSet fires events whenever its data changes).

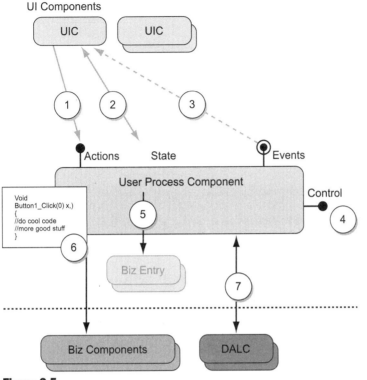

Figure 2.5
User process component design

- **Control functions that let you start, pause, restart, and cancel a particular user process (4)**. These functions should be kept separate, but can be intermixed with the user process actions. For example, the code sample discussed earlier contains SaveToDataBase and ResumeCheckout methods. Control methods could load required reference data for the UI (such as the information needed to fill a combo box) from data access logic components (7) or delegate this work to the user interface component (forms, controls, ASP.NET pages) that needs the data.

General Recommendations for User Process Components

When designing user process components, consider the following recommendations:

- Decide whether you need to manage user processes as components that are separate from your user interface implementation. Separate user processes are most needed in applications with a high number of user interface dialog boxes, or in applications in which the user processes may be subject to customization and may benefit from a plug-in approach.

- Choose where to store the state of the user process:
  - If the process is running in a connected fashion, store interim state for long-running processes in a central SQL Server database; in disconnected scenarios, store it in local XML files, isolated storage, or local Microsoft SQL Server™ 2000 Desktop Engine (MSDE) databases. On Pocket PC devices, you can store state in a SQL Server CE database.
  - If the process is not long-running and does not need to be recovered in case of a problem, you should persist the state in memory. For user interfaces built for rich clients, you may want to keep the state in memory. For Web applications, you may choose to store the user process state in the Session object of ASP.NET. If you are running in a Web farm, you should store the session in a central state server or a SQL Server database. ASP.NET will clean up SQL Server-stored session to prevent the buildup of stale data.
- Design your user process components so that they are serializable. This will help you implement any persistence scheme.
- Include exception handling in user process components, and propagate exceptions to the user interface. Exceptions that are thrown by the user process components should be caught by user interface components and published as described in Chapter 3: Security, Operational Management, and Communications Policies."

Network Connectivity and Offline Applications

In many cases, your application will require support for offline operations when network connectivity is unavailable. For example, many mobile applications, including rich clients for Pocket PC or Table PC devices, must be able to function when the user is disconnected from the corporate network. Offline applications must rely on local data and user process state to perform their work. When designing offline applications, follow the general guidelines in the following discussion.

The online and offline status should be displayed to the user. This is usually done in status bars or title bars or with visual cues around user interface elements that require a connection to the server.

The development of most of the application user interface should be reusable, with little or no modification needed to support offline scenarios. While offline, your application will not have:

- Access to online data returned by data access logic components.
- The ability to invoke business processes synchronously. As a result, the application will not know whether the call succeeded or be able to use any returned data.

If your application does not implement a fully message-based interface to your servers but relies on synchronously acquiring data and knowing the results of business processes (as most of today's applications do), you should do the following to provide the illusion of connectivity:

- Implement a local cache for read-only reference data that relates to the user's activities. You can then implement an offline data access logic component that implements exactly the same queries as your server-side data access logic components but accesses the local storage. You can implement the local cache as a desktop MSDE database. This enables you to reuse the design and implementation of your main SQL Server schemas and stored procedures. However, MSDE affects the global state of the computer it is installed on, and you may have trouble accessing it from applications configured for semi-trust. In many scenarios, using MSDE may be overkill for your state persistence requirements, and storing data in an XML file or persisted dataset may be a better solution.

- Implement an offline business component that has the same interface as your business components, but takes the submitted data and places it in a store-and-forward, reliable messaging system such as Message Queuing. This offline component may then return nothing or a preset value to its caller.

- Implement UI functionality that provides a way to inspect the business action "outbox" and possibly delete messages in it. If Message Queuing is used to queue offline messages, you will need to set the correct permissions on the queue to do this from your application.

- Design your application's transactions to accommodate message-based UI interactions. You will have to take extra care to manage optimistic locking and the results of transactions based on stale data. A common technique for performing updates is to submit both the old and new data, and to let the related business process or data access logic component eventually resolve any conflicts. For business processes, the submission may include critical reference data that the business logic uses to decide whether or not to let the data through. For example, you can include product prices alongside product IDs and quantities when submitting an order. For a more detailed discussion of optimistic locking, see "Designing Data Tier Components and Passing Data Through Tiers" on MSDN (*http://msdn.microsoft.com/library/?url=/library/en-us/dnbda/html/ BOAGag.asp?frame=true*).

- Let the user persist the state of the application's user processes to disk and resume them later.

The advent of mobile devices based on IP networking, wireless security standard evolution, the 802.11 standard, IPv6, the Tablet PC, and other technologies will make wireless networks more popular. The issue with wireless networks is that with today's technology, they cannot guarantee connectivity with high confidence in all areas. For example, building structure, nearby machinery, and other factors may cause permanent and transient "dark zones" in the network. If you are designing an application for use in a wireless environment, consider designing it as a message-based, offline application, to prevent an experience full of exceptions and retries. For example, you could design an application so that an offline user can enter data through the same user interface as when connected, and the data can be stored in a local database or queued and synchronized later, when the user reconnects. SQL Server supports replication, which can be used to automate the synchronization of data in a loosely coupled fashion, allowing data to be downloaded to the offline device while connected, modified while disconnected, and resynchronized when reconnected. Microsoft Message Queuing allows data to be encapsulated in a message and queued on the disconnected device for submission to a server-side queue when connected. Components of the server will then read the message from the queue and process it. Using local queues or SQL Server replication to handle communication of user input to the server can help mitigate connectivity issues, even when the application is nominally connected. Where a more tightly coupled approach is required, you should use transactions and custom logging to ensure data integrity.

When data synchronization occurs between a disconnected (or loosely coupled) application and a server, you must take into account the following security considerations:

- Message Queuing provides its own authorization model, based on Windows authentication. If your application relies on custom, application-managed authentication, your client-side components will need to sign the documents that are submitted to the server.

- The client cannot be impersonated on the server if data is submitted through a queue.

- If SQL Server replication is used, you may need to specify an account with permission to access the SQL Server databases on the server. When replicating from SQL Server CE on a mobile device, a secure connection to the Internet Information Services (IIS) site containing the SQL Server CE Server Agent must be established. For more information about configuring SQL Server replication, see the documentation supplied with SQL Server and SQL Server CE.

- If network communication takes place over an HTTP connection, you may want to use Secure Sockets Layer (SSL) to secure the channel.

Notification to Users and Business Process-to-User Communication

Your application may be required to notify users about specific events. As the communication capabilities of the Internet grow, you will have more options for notifying users. Common technologies currently include e-mail, instant messaging, cell phone messaging, paging, and so on.

Instant notification may involve many possible notification technologies and the use of presence services to detect the appropriate way to contact a user. Microsoft Patterns & Practices has released a reference architecture that covers this scenario. It is available on MSDN at *http://msdn.microsoft.com/library/en-us/dnenra/html /enraelp.asp*.

Designing Business Layers

The core of your application is the business functionality it provides. An application performs a business process that consists of one or more tasks. In the simplest cases, each task can be encapsulated in a method of a.NET component, and called synchronously or asynchronously. For more complex business processes that require multiple steps and long running transactions, the application needs to have some way of orchestrating the business tasks and storing state until the process has completed. In these scenarios, you can use BizTalk Server Orchestration to define the workflow for the business process. The BizTalk Server schedule that implements the workflow can then use BizTalk Server messaging functionality or call your .NET business components to perform each task as it is required.

You can design the logic in your business layers to be used directly by presentation components or to be encapsulated as a service and called through a service interface, which coordinates the asynchronous conversation with the service's callers and invokes the BizTalk Server workflow or business components. The core of the business logic is sometimes also referred to as *domain* logic. Your business components may also make requests of external services, in which case you may need to implement service agents to manage the conversation required for the particular business task performed by each service you need to use.

Figure 2.6 on the next page shows the business layers of an application.

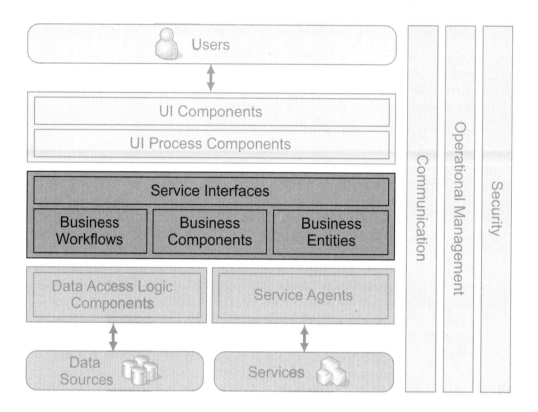

Figure 2.6
Business component layers

Business Components and Workflows

When implementing business functionality, you have to decide if you need to orchestrate the business process or if a set of business components will be sufficient.

You should use business workflows (implemented with BizTalk Orchestration) to:

- Manage a process that involves multiple steps and long-running transactions.
- Expose an interface that implements a business process enabling your application to engage in a conversation or contract with other services.
- Take advantage of the broad range of adaptors and connectors for multiple technologies that are available for BizTalk Server.

You can implement the business process using only business components when:

- You do not need to maintain conversation state beyond the business activity, and the business functionality can be implemented as a single atomic transaction.
- You need to encapsulate functionality and logic that can be reused from many business processes.
- The business logic that needs to be implemented is computationally intensive or needs fine-grained control of data structures and APIs.
- You need to have fine-grained control over data and flow of logic.

In the retail example, the process of placing an order involves multiple steps (authorizing the credit card, processing payment, arranging delivery, and so on), and these steps need to be performed in a particular sequence. The most appropriate design approach for this kind of business process is to create business components to encapsulate each individual step in the process and to orchestrate those components using a business workflow.

Designing Business Components

Business components can be the root of atomic transactions. They implement business rules in diverse patterns and accept and return simple or complex data structures. Your business components should expose functionality in a way that is agnostic to the data stores and services needed to perform the work, and should be composed in meaningful and transactionally consistent ways.

Business logic will usually evolve and grow, providing higher-level operations and logic that encapsulates pre-existing logic. In many cases, you will need to compose pre-existing business functionality in order to perform the required business logic. When composing business logic, you must take special care when transactions are involved.

If your business process will be invoking other business processes in the context of an atomic transaction, all the invoked business processes must ensure their operations participate in the existing transaction so that their operations will roll back if the calling business logic aborts. It should be safe to retry any atomic operation if it fails without fear of making data inconsistent. You can think of a transaction boundary as a retry boundary. Transactions across servers running Windows can be managed using Distributed Transaction Coordinator (DTC), which is used by .NET Enterprise Services (COM+). To manage distributed transactions in heterogeneous environments, you can use COM Transaction Integrator (COMTI) and Host Integration Server 2000. For more information about COMTI and Host Integration Server, see *http://www.microsoft.com/hiserver*.

If you cannot implement atomic transactions, you will need to provide compensating methods and processes. Note that a compensating action does not necessarily roll back all application data to the previous state, but rather restores the business data to a consistent state. For example, if you are a supplier, you may expose a B2B shopping interface to partners. A compensating action for canceling an order being processed may involve charging an order cancellation fee. For long-running transactions and processes, the compensating action may be different at different states in the workflow, so you need to design these for appropriate stages in the process.

For information about handling transactions and isolation level issues, see "Transactions" in ".NET Data Access Architecture Guide" on MSDN (*http:// msdn.microsoft.com/library/en-us/dnbda/html/daag.asp*).

The following list summarizes the recommendations for designing business components:

- Rely on message-based communication as much as possible.

- Ensure that processes exposed through service interfaces are idempotent, meaning that your application or service will not reach an inconsistent state if the same message is received twice.

- Choose transaction boundaries carefully so that retries and composition are possible. This applies to both atomic and long-running transactions. You should also consider using retries for message-based systems, especially when exposing your application functionality as a service.

- Business components should be able to run as much as possible in the context of any service user—not necessarily impersonating a specific application user. This lets you invoke them with mechanisms that do not transmit or delegate user identity.

- Choose and keep a consistent data format (such as XML, DataSet, and so on) for input parameters and return values.

- Set transaction isolation levels appropriately. For information about handling transactions and isolation level issues, see "Transactions" in ".NET Data Access Architecture Guide" on MSDN (*http://msdn.microsoft.com/library/en-us/dnbda/html /daag.asp*).

Implementing Business Components with .NET

You can create components that encapsulate your business logic using the .NET Framework. Your managed code can take advantage of Enterprise Services (COM+) for distributed transactions and other services commonly needed in distributed applications.

Your business components:

- Are invoked by the user process layer, service interfaces, and other business processes, typically with some business data to operate on, expressed as a complex data structure (a document).

- Are the root of transactions, and therefore must vote in the transactions they participate in.
- Should validate input and output.
- May expose compensating operations for the business processes they provide.
- May call data access logic components to retrieve and/or update application data.
- May call external services through service agents.
- May call other business components and initiate business workflows.
- May raise an exception to the caller if something goes wrong when dealing with atomic transactions.
- May use the features of Enterprise Services for initiating and voting on heterogeneous transactions. You need to consider the fact that different transaction options can have a great impact on performance. However, transaction management is not an adjustment mechanism or variable for improving application performance. For performance comparisons of different transaction approaches, see "Performance Comparison: Transaction Control" on MSDN (*http:// msdn.microsoft.com/library/en-us/Dnbda/html/Bdadotnetarch13.asp*). Your transactional settings can be:
  - **Required**. Use this option for components that may be the root of a transaction, or that will participate in existing transactions.
  - **Supported**. Use this option for components that do not necessarily require a transaction, but that you want to participate in an existing transaction if one exists.
  - **RequiresNew**. Use this option when you want the component to start a new transaction that is independent of existing transactions.
  - **NotSupported**. Use this option when you do not want the component to participate in transactions.

Note: Using the **RequiresNew** and **NotSupported** options will affect transaction composability, so you need to be aware of the impact of retrying a parent transaction.

Business components are called by the following consumers:
- Service interfaces
- User process components
- Business workflows
- Other business components

Figure 2.7 shows a typical business component interacting with data access logic components, service interfaces, service agents, and other business components.

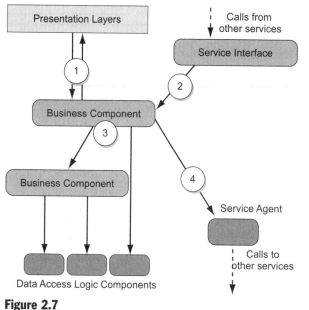

Figure 2.7
Business components

Note the following points in Figure 2.7:

1. Business components can be invoked by components in the presentation layers (typically user process components) or by business workflows (not shown).

2. Business components can also be invoked by service interfaces (for example, an XML Web service or a Message Queuing listener function.

3. Business components call data access logic components to retrieve and update data, and they can also invoke other business components.

4. Business components can also invoke service agents. You need to take extra care in designing compensation logic in case the service you are accessing is unavailable or takes a long time to return a response.

Note: The arrows in Figure 2.7 represent control flow, not data flow.

When to Use Enterprise Services for Your Business Components

Enterprise Services (COM+) is the obvious choice for a host environment for your business components. Enterprise Services provide your components with role-based security, heterogeneous transaction control, object pooling, and message-based interfaces for your components by means of Queued Components (among other things). You may choose not to use Enterprise Services in an application, but for anything more than simple operations against a single data source, you will need its services, and taking advantage of the model provided by Enterprise Services early on provides a smoother growth path for your system.

You should decide at the very beginning of the design process whether or not to use Enterprise Services when implementing your business components, because it will be more difficult to add or remove Enterprise Services features from your component design and code after it is built.

When implementing components with Enterprise Services, you need to be aware of the following design characteristics:

- **Remoting channel restriction**. Only HTTP and DCOM-RPC channels are supported. For more information, see "Designing the Communications Policy" in Chapter 3, "Security, Operational Management, and Communications Policies."

- **Strong-named components**: You need to sign these components and all components they use in turn.

- **Deployment**. Your components will either be self registering (in which case they will require administrative rights at run time), or you will need to perform a special deployment step. However, most server-side components require extra deployment steps anyway (to register Event Log sources, create Message Queuing queues, and so on).

- **Security**. You will need to choose whether to use the Enterprise Services role model, which is based on Windows authentication, or to just use .NET-based security.

For more information about Enterprise Services, see "Understanding Enterprise Services (COM+) in.NET" on MSDN (*http://msdn.microsoft.com/library/en-us/dndotnet /html/entserv.asp*).

Commonly Used Patterns for Business Components

Regardless of whether your business components are hosted in Enterprise Services, there are many common patterns for implementing business tasks in your code. Commonly used patterns include:

- **Pipeline pattern**. Actions and queries are executed on a component in a sequential manner.

  A pipeline is a definition of steps that are executed to perform a business function. All steps are executed sequentially. Each step may involve reading or writing to data confirming the "pipeline state," and may or may not access an external service. When invoking an asynchronous service as part of a step, a pipeline can wait until a response is returned (if a response is expected), or proceed to the next step in the pipeline if the response is not required in order to continue processing.

Use the pipeline pattern when:

- You can specify the sequence of a known set of steps.
- You do not need to wait for an asynchronous response from each step.
- You want all downstream components to be able to inspect and act on data that comes from upstream (but not vice versa).

Advantages of the pipeline pattern include:

- It is simple to understand and implement.
- It enforces sequential processing.
- It is easy to wrap in an atomic transaction.

Disadvantages of the pipeline pattern include:

- The pattern may be too simplistic, especially for service orchestration in which you need to branch the execution of the business logic in complex ways.
- It does not handle conditional constructs, loops, and other flow control logic well. Adding one step affects the performance of every execution of the pipeline.

The pipeline pattern is used extensively in applications based on Microsoft Commerce Server. For more information about how pipelines are used with Commerce Server, see "Pipeline Programming Concepts" in the Commerce Server 2000 SDK documentation on MSDN (*http://msdn.microsoft.com/library /en-us/comsrv2k/htm/cs_sp_pipelineobj_woce.asp*).

- **Event pattern**. Events are fired under particular business conditions, and code is written to respond to those events.

   You use the event pattern when you want to have many activities happen but all receive the same starting data and cannot communicate with each other. Activities may execute in parallel or sequentially. Different implementations of the event may or may not run, depending on specific filtering information. If the implementations are set to run sequentially, order cannot be guaranteed.

   Use the event pattern when:

   - You want to be able to manage independent and isolated implementations of a specific 'function' independently.
   - Responses from one implementation do not affect the way another implementation works.
   - All implementations are write only or fire-and-forget, where the output of the business process is defined by none of the implementations, or by just one specific business implementation.

Advantages of the event pattern include:

- Maintainability is improved by keeping unrelated business process independent.
- It encourages parallel processing, which may result in performance benefits.
- It is easy to wrap in an atomic transaction.
- It is agnostic to whether implementations run asynchronously or synchronously because no reply is expected.

Disadvantages of the event pattern include:

- It does not let you build complex responses for the business function.
- A component cannot use the data or status of another component in the event pattern to perform its work.

Enterprise Services provides the Events service, which provides a good starting point implementation of the event pattern. For more information about Enterprise Services Events, see "COM+ Events" in the COM+ SDK documentation on MSDN (*http://msdn.microsoft.com/library/en-us/cossdk/htm/ pgservices_events_2y9f.asp*).

Implementing Business Workflows with BizTalk Server

When your business processes require multiple steps or long-running transactions, you need to manage the workflow, handling conversation state and exchanging messages with diverse services as required. BizTalk Server includes orchestration services that help meet these challenges.

You can design your business processes using BizTalk Server Orchestration services, and create XLANG schedules that implement your business functionality. XLANG schedules are created graphically using BizTalk Server Orchestration Designer and can use BizTalk Messaging Services, .NET components, COM components, Message Queuing, or script to perform business tasks. XLANG schedules can be used to implement long-running transactions, and they automatically persist their state in a SQL Server database.

You can use BizTalk Server Orchestration to implement most kinds of business functionality. However, it is particularly suitable when your business process involves long-running workflow processes in which business documents are exchanged between multiple services. Documents can be submitted to BizTalk Server programmatically, or they can be delivered to a monitored file system folder or message queue known as a receive function. Receive functions ensure that the delivered documents match the specification defined for expected business documents, and if so, they consume the document and submit it to the appropriate business process channel in BizTalk Server. From this point of view, a receive function can be thought of as a simple form of service interface.

For an in-depth example that shows how to implement a business process using BizTalk Server Orchestration and Visual Studio .NET, see "Building a Scalable Business Process Automation Engine Using BizTalk Server 2002 and Visual Studio .NET" on MSDN (*http://msdn.microsoft.com/library/en-us/dnbiz2k2/html/ BizTalkVSautoeng.asp*).

When your business process involves interactions with existing systems, such as mainframe applications, BizTalk Server can use adapters to integrate with them. For more information about integrating BizTalk Server with existing systems, see "Legacy File Integration Using Microsoft BizTalk Server 2000" on MSDN (*http:// msdn.microsoft.com/library/en-us/dnbiz/html/legacyfileint.asp*).

BizTalk Server Orchestration Implementation

Figure 2.8 shows how an orchestrated business process interacts with service interfaces, service agents, and business components.

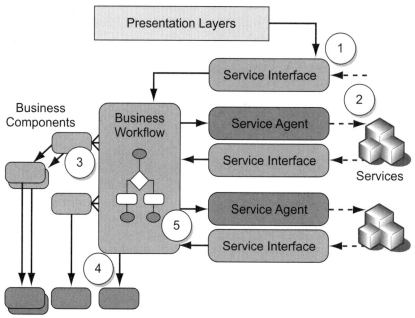

Data Access Logic Components

Figure 2.8
An orchestrated business process

Note the following points in Figure 2.8:

1. Business workflows can be invoked from other services or from the presentation components (usually from user process components) using the service interface.

2. A business workflow invokes other services through a service agent, or directly through the service interfaces. Every outgoing message does not necessarily need to match an incoming message. You can implement service interfaces and service

agents in code, or if only simple operations are required, you can use the message transformation and functoid features of BizTalk Server.

3. Business workflows invoke business components. The business workflow or the components that it invokes can initiate atomic transactions.

4. Business workflows invoke data access logic components to perform data-related activities.

5. When designing business workflows, you must consider long response times, or method invocations with no reply at all. BizTalk Server automatically allows for long running conversations with external services.

BizTalk Server Orchestration schedules are created graphically using the BizTalk Server Orchestration Designer. Figure 2.9 shows how an orchestration flow in the previous figure would look as rendered by Microsoft Visio® drawing and diagramming software. Notice how similar the conceptual diagram in Figure 2.9 looks to the flow a business analyst and developer needs to work with.

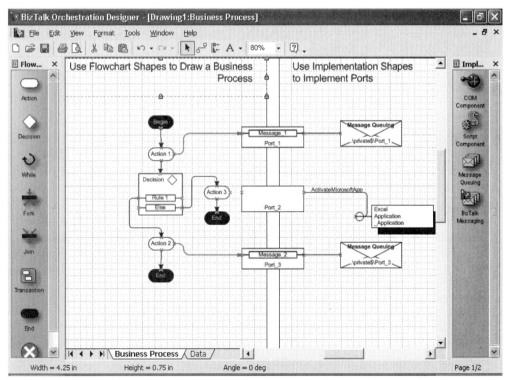

Figure 2.9
An orchestration flow in BizTalk Server Orchestration Designer

The drawing is then compiled into an XLANG schedule, which is an XML format file containing the instructions necessary for BizTalk Server to perform the tasks in the business process.

After it is compiled, the schedule can be initiated in one of the following ways:

● A BizTalk Server message can be submitted to BizTalk Server programmatically or through a file system or Message Queuing receive function.

● A schedule can be started programmatically from COM-based code using the *sked* moniker.

For more information about BizTalk Server Orchestration, read *BizTalk Server:The Complete Reference* by David Lowe et al (published by Osborne/McGraw Hill) and "Designing BizTalk Orchestrations" in the BizTalk Server 2000 documentation (*http://msdn.microsoft.com/library/en-us/biztalks/htm/lat_sched_intro_xiju.asp*).

For information about adapters for BizTalk:

http://www.microsoft.com/biztalk/evaluation/adapters/adapterslist.asp

The BizTalk Server Adapter's Developer Guide can be found at:

http://www.microsoft.com/biztalk/techinfo/development/wp_adapterdevelopersguide.asp

Designing a Service Interface

If you are exposing business functionality as a service, you need to provide an entry point for your clients to call that abstracts the internal implementation. You may also need to expose similar functionality to different callers with different authentication requirements and service level agreement (SLA) commitments. You can provide an entry point to your service by creating a service interface.

A service interface is a software entity typically implemented as a façade that handles mapping and transformation services to allow communication with a service, and enforces a process and a policy for communication. A service interface exposes methods, which may be called individually or in a specific sequence to form a conversation that implements a business task. For example, the credit card service in the retail application scenario might provide a method named AuthorizeCard that verifies credit card details, and a second method named ProcessPayment that transfers funds from the cardholder's account to the retailer. These steps would be performed in the appropriate sequence to process an order payment

The necessary communication format, data schema, security requirements, and process are determined as part of a contract, which is published by the service. This contract provides the information clients need to locate and communicate with the service interface.

When designing service interfaces, consider the following:

● Think of a service interface as a trust boundary for your application.

● If your service interfaces are exposed to external organizations and consumers, or made publicly available, you should design them in such a way that changes to your internal implementation will not require a change to the service interface.

- The same business logic in your service may need to be consumed in different ways by different clients, so you may need to publish multiple service interfaces for the same functionality.

- Different service interfaces may define different communication channels, message formats, authentication mechanisms, performance service level agreements, and transactional capabilities. Common service level agreements are defined in time to respond to a certain request with a certain amount of information.

You can implement service interfaces in different ways, depending on how you want to expose the functionality of your application or service:

- To expose your business logic as an XML Web service, you can use ASP.NET Web service pages or expose some components through .NET remoting using SOAP and HTTP.

- To expose your service's functionality to clients sending Message Queuing messages, you can use Message Queuing Triggers or Enterprise Services Queued Components, or you can write your own 'message receiving' services.

For more information, see "Designing the Communications Policy" in Chapter 3, "Security, Operational Management, and Communications Policies."

Service Interface Characteristics

Consider the following design characteristics of service interfaces:

- Sometimes the .NET infrastructure will let you use a transparent service interface (for example, you can expose Enterprise Services objects as Web services in Windows .NET Server), and sometimes you may need to add specific artifacts to your application, such as XML Web services, BizTalk Orchestration workflows, or messaging ports. Consider the impact of using transparent service interfaces, because they may not provide the abstraction necessary to facilitate changes to the business functionality at a later date without affecting the service interface. Implementing façades has its development cost, but will help you to isolate changes and to make your application more maintainable.

- Service interfaces can implement caching, mapping, and simple format and schema transformations; however, these façades should not implement business logic.

- The service interface may involve a transactional transport (for example, Message Queuing) or a non-transactional transport (for example, XML Web services over HTTP). This will affect your error and transaction management strategy.

- You should design service interfaces for maximum interoperability with other platforms and services, relying whenever possible on industry standards for communications, security, and formats, standard or simple message formats (for example, simple XML schemas for XML Web services), and non-platform specific authentication mechanisms.

- Sometimes the service interface will have a security identity of its own, and will authenticate the incoming messages but will not be able to impersonate them. You should consider using this approach when calling business components that are deployed on a different server from the service interface.

Using Business Façades with Service Interfaces

The channel or communication mechanism you use to expose your business logic as a service may have an associated way of implementing the service interface code. For example, if you choose to build Web services, most of your service interface logic will reside in the Web service itself, namely the asmx.cs files. You could also expose your service through Message Queuing, in which case you could use Queued Components from Enterprise Services, custom listeners, or Message Queuing Triggers to "fire up" the component that acts as service interface.

If you are planning to build a system that may be invoked through different mechanisms, you should add a façade between the business logic and the service interface. By implementing this façade, you can consolidate in one place your policy-related code (such as authorization, auditing, validations, and so on) so it can be reused across multiple service interfaces that deal with diverse channels. This façade provides extra maintainability because it isolates changes in the communication mechanisms from the implementation of the business components. The service interface code then only deals with the specifics of the communication mechanism or channel (for example, examining Web service SOAP headers or getting information from Message Queuing messages) and sets the proper context for invoking the business façade component. Figure 2.10 shows a business façade used in this manner.

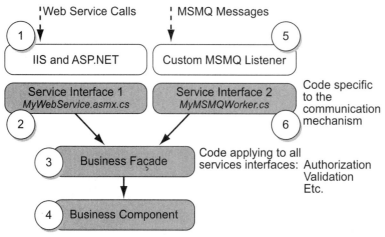

Figure 2.10
Using a business façade with service interfaces

Figure 2.10 shows an example of how a business façade is used with the service interfaces of a system. IIS and ASP.NET receive an HTTP call (1) and invoke a Web service interface named *MyWebService.asmx* (2). This service interface inspects some SOAP message headers, and sets the correct principal object based on the authentication of the Web service. It then invokes a business façade component (3) that validates, authorizes, and audits the call. The façade then invokes a business component that performs the business work (4). Later the system is required to support Message Queuing, so a custom listener is built (5) that picks up messages and invokes a service interface component named *MyMSMQWorker* (6). This service interface component extracts data off the Message Queuing message properties (such as Body, Label, and so on) and also sets the correct principal object on the thread based on the Message Queuing message signature. It then invokes the business façade. By factoring the code of the business façade out of the service interface, the application was able to add a communication mechanism with much less effort.

Transaction Management in Service Interfaces

Your service interface will need to deal with a channel that provides transactional capabilities (such as Message Queuing) or one that doesn't (such as XML Web services). It is very important that you design your transaction boundaries so that operations can be retried in face of an error. To do so, make sure that all the resources you use are transactional, mark your root component as "requires transaction," and mark all sub components as either "requires transaction" or "supports transactions."

With transactional messaging mechanisms, the service interface starts the transaction first and then picks up the message. If the transaction rolls back, the message is automatically "unreceived" and is placed back in the queue for a retry. When using Message Queuing, Enterprise Services Queued Components, or Message Queuing Triggers, you can define a message queue-and-receive operation as transactional to achieve this automatically.

If you are using a messaging mechanism that is not transactional (such as XML Web services), you need to call the root of the transaction from the code in the service interface. In the case of a failure, you can design the service interface code to retry the operation or return to the caller an appropriate exception or preset data representing a failure.

Representing Data and Passing It Through Tiers

When your data access logic components return data, they can do so in a number of formats. These formats can vary from the data-centric (for example, an XML string) to the more object oriented (for example, a custom component that encapsulates an instance of a business entity). Common formats for returning data are:

- XML
- DataReader
- DataSet
- Typed DataSet
- Custom object with properties that map to data fields, and methods that perform data modifications through data access logic components.

For more information about the choices of data formats available in your application design, see "Designing Data Tier Components and Passing Data Through Tiers" on MSDN (*http://msdn.microsoft.com/library/?url=/library/en-us/dnbda/html/BOAGag.asp?frame=true*).

The data format you choose to use depends on how you want to work with the data. It is recommended that you avoid designs requiring you to transfer data in a custom object-oriented format, because doing so requires custom serialization implementation and can create a performance overhead. Generally, you should use a more data-centric format, such as a DataSet, to pass the data from the data access logic components to the business layers, and then use it to hydrate a custom business entity if you want to work with the data in an object-oriented fashion. In many cases, though, it will be simpler just to work with the business data in a DataSet.

Representing Data with Custom Business Entity Components

In most cases, you should work with data directly by using ADO.NET datasets or XML documents. This allows you to pass structured data between the layers of your application without having to write any custom code. However, if you want to encapsulate all the details about working with a particular format, or you want to add behaviors to your data, you may need to develop custom components. This gives you tight control over what other application components can do with the data, allows you to abstract internal formats from the data schema that the application uses, and enables you to add behavior to your data. This guide refers to the components you use to represent data as *business entities*.

For example, the ordering process discussed earlier in this guide could use an Order object, which has an associated Customer object, and a collection of LineItem objects. These components form part of the business layers of your application, and can be consumed by other business components or by presentation components.

Entity components contain snapshot data. They are effectively a local cache of information, so the data can only be guaranteed to be consistent if it is read in the context of an active transaction. You should not map one business entity to each database table; typically a business entity will have a schema that is a denormalization of underlying schemas. Note that the entity may represent data that has been aggregated from many sources.

Because the component stores data values and exposes them through its properties, it provides stateful programmatic access to the business data and related functionality. You should avoid designing your business entity components in such a way that the data store is accessed each time a property changes and should instead provide an Update method that propagates all local changes back to the database. Business entity components should not access the database directly, but should use data access logic components to perform data-related work as their methods are called. Business entities should not initiate any kind of transactions, and should not use data access APIs—they are just a representation of data, potentially with behavior. Because they may be called from business components as well as user interfaces, they should flow transactions transparently and should not vote on any ongoing transaction.

You may want to design your business entity components to be serializable, allowing you to persist current state (for example, to store on a local disk if working offline, or into a Message Queuing message).

Business entity components simplify the transition between object-oriented programming and document-based development models. Object-oriented design is common in stateful environments such as user interface design, whereas business functionality and transactions can typically be expressed more clearly in terms of document exchanges.

Note: Custom business entity components are not a mandatory part of all applications. Many solutions (especially ASP.NET-based applications and business components) do not use custom representations of business entities, but instead use DataSets or XML documents because they provide all the required information and the development model is more task- and document- based as opposed to object-oriented.

Business Entity Component Interface Design

Business entity components expose:

- Property accessors (get and set functions) for attributes of the entity.
- Collection accessors for sub collections of related data. (The collections don't necessarily yield collections of business entities, so you can design your service entity to expose DataSets or DataTables directly and not be concerned about object model traversal.)

- Control functions and properties commonly used in entity management, for example, Load, Save, IsDirty, and Validate.
- Methods to access metadata for the entity, which can be useful in improving maintainability of the user interface.
- Events to signal changes in the underlying data.
- Methods to perform business tasks or get data for complex queries. These methods may act on the local data only (for example, Order.GetTotalCost) or on the business components and processes (for example, Order.Place).
- Methods and interfaces needed for data binding.

Consumers of business entity components include:

- User interaction components for rich clients. These components may bind to the data in business entities or the data exposed by any queries the component may expose. UI controller functions may also set and get properties of business entities for data input and display.
- User process components. User process components may hold one or more business entities as part of their internal business-specific state.
- Business components. Business processes may pass a business entity as a parameter to a data access logic component method (for example, an Order object could be passed to an InsertOrder method in a data access logic component). Alternatively, business components could also use business entities to access data behavior (for example by calling a Place method on the Order object, which in turn passes the order data to a data access logic component), but this approach is more uncommon than passing the business entity directly to a data access logic component method because it mixes a functional, document-oriented model with an object-based model.

Recommendations for Business Entity Design

These recommendations will help you implement the right mechanism to represent your data:

- Carefully consider whether you need custom entity coding or whether other data representations work for your requirements. Coding custom entities is a complex task that increases in development cost with the number of features it provides. Typically, custom entities are implemented for applications that need to expose a custom macro or a developer-friendly scripting object model for customization.
- Implement business entities by deriving them from a base class that provides boilerplate functionality and encapsulates common tasks.
- Rely on keeping internal datasets or XML documents for complex data instead of internal collections, structs, and so on.

- Implement a common set of interfaces across your business entities that expose common sets of functionality:
  - Control methods and properties, such as Save, Load, Delete, IsDirty, and Validate.
  - Metadata methods, such as getAttributesMetadata, getChildDatasetsMetadata, and getRelatedEntitiesMetadata. This is especially useful for user interface design.
- Isolate validation rules as metadata, for example by exposing XML Schema Definition Language (XSD) schemas. Make sure, however, that external callers cannot tamper with these validation rules.
- Business entities should validate the data they encapsulate through the enforcement of continuous and point-in-time validation rules.
- Implement an implicit enforcement of relationships between entities based on the data schema and the business rules around the data. For example, an Order object could have a maximum number of LineItem references.
- Design business entities to rely on data access logic components for database interaction. Doing so allows you to implement all your data access policies and related business logic in one place. If your business entities access SQL Server databases directly, it will mean that applications deployed to clients that use the business entities will need SQL connectivity and logon permissions.

For detailed design recommendations and sample code that will assist you when developing your business entity components, see "Designing Data Tier Components and Passing Data Through Tiers" on MSDN (*http://msdn.microsoft.com/library /?url=/library/en-us/dnbda/html/BOAGag.asp?frame=true*).

Designing Data Layers

Almost all applications and services need to store and access some kind of data. For example, the retail application discussed in this guide needs to store product, customer, and order data.

When working with data, you need to determine:

- The data store you are using.
- The design of the components used to access the data store.
- The format of the data passed between components, and the programming model it requires.

Your application or service may have one or more data sources, and these data sources may be of different types. The logic used to access data in a data source will be encapsulated in *data access logic components*, which provide methods for querying and updating data. The data your application logic needs to work is related to real-world *entities* that play a part in your business. In some scenarios, you may have custom components representing these entities, while in others you may choose to work with data by using ADO.NET datasets or XML documents directly.

Figure 2.11 shows how the logical data layer of an application consists of one or more data stores, and depicts a layer of data access logic components that are used to retrieve and manipulate the data in those data stores.

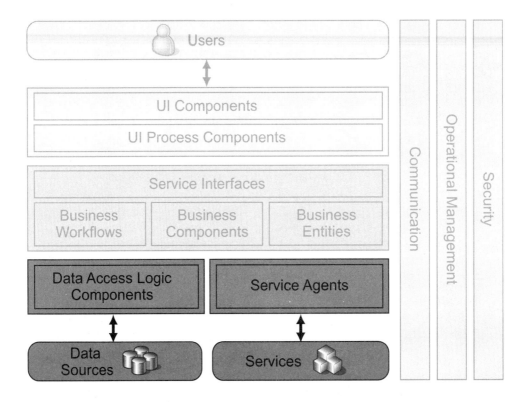

Figure 2.11
Data components

Most applications use a relational database as the primary data store for application data. Other choices include the Microsoft Exchange Server Web store, legacy databases, the file system, or document management services.

When your application retrieves data from the database, it may do so using a data format such as a DataSet or DataReader. The data will then be transferred across the layers and tiers of the application and finally will be operated on by one of your components. You may want to use different data formats for retrieving, passing, and operating on the data; for example, you might use the data in a DataSet to populate properties in a custom entity object. However, you should strive to keep the formats consistent, because it will probably improve the performance and maintainability of the application to have only a limited set of formats, avoiding the need for extra translation layers and the need to learn different APIs.

The following sections discuss the choice of data stores, the design of data access logic components, and the choices available for representing data.

Data Stores

Common types of stores include:

- **Relational databases**. Relational databases such as SQL Server databases provide high volume, transactional, high performance data management with security, operations, and data transformation capabilities. Relational databases also host complex data logic instructions and functions in the form of stored procedures that can be used as an efficient environment for data-intensive business processes. SQL Server also provides a desktop and palm-held device version that lets you use transparent implementations for data access logic components. Database design is beyond the scope of this guide. For relational database design information, see "Database Design Considerations" in the SQL Server 2000 SDK (*http:// msdn.microsoft.com/library/default.asp?url=/library/en-us /createdb/cm_8_des_02_62ur.asp*)

- **Messaging databases**. You can store data in the Exchange Server Web store. This is useful especially if your application is groupware-, workgroup-, or messaging-centric and you don't want to rely on other data stores that may need to be managed separately. However, messaging data stores typically have lower performance, scalability, availability, and management capabilities than fully fledged relational database management systems (RDBMS), and it is therefore relatively uncommon for applications to use the data store provided in a messaging product. For information about developing an Exchange Server-based data store, see "Developing Web Storage System Applications" on MSDN (*http:// msdn.microsoft.com/library/en-us/dnmes2k/html/webstorewp.asp*).

- **File system**. You may decide to store your data in your own files in the file system. These files could be in your own format or in an XML format with a schema defined for the purposes of the application.

There are many other stores (such as XML databases, online analytical processing services, data warehousing databases, and so on) but they are beyond the scope of this guide.

Data Access Logic Components

Regardless of the data store you choose, your application or service will use data access logic components to access the data. These components abstract the semantics of the underlying data store and data access technology (such as ADO.NET), and provide a simple programmatic interface for retrieving and performing operations on data.

Data access logic components usually implement a stateless design pattern that separates the business processing from the data access logic. Each data access logic component typically provides methods to perform Create, Read, Update, and Delete (CRUD) operations relating to a specific business entity in the application (for example, order). These methods may be used by the business processes. Specific queries can be used by your user interface to render reference data (such as a list of valid credit card types).

When your application contains multiple data access logic components, it can be useful to use a generic data access helper component to manage database connections, execute commands, cache parameters, and so on. The data access logic components provide the logic required to access specific business data, while the generic data access helper utility component centralizes data access API development and data connection configuration, and helps to reduce code duplication.
A well designed data access helper component should have no negative impact on performance, and provides a central place for data access tuning and optimization. Microsoft provides the Data Access Application Block for .NET (*http:// msdn.microsoft.com/library/en-us/dnbda/html/daab-rm.asp*), which can be used as a generic data access helper utility component in your applications when using SQL Server databases.

Figure 2.12 shows the use of data access logic components to access data.

Note the following points in Figure 2.12:

1. Data access logic components expose methods for inserting, deleting, updating, and retrieving data. This includes the provision of paging functionality when retrieving large quantities of data.

2. You can use a data access helper component to centralize connection management and all code that deals with a specific data source.

3. You should implement your queries and data operations as stored procedures (if supported by the data source) to enhance performance and maintainability.

Note: Data access logic components are recommended for all applications that need to access business data (such as products, orders, and so on). However, other products and technologies may use databases to store their own operational data, without the need for custom data access logic components.

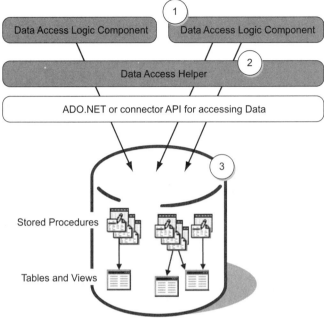

Figure 2.12
Data access logic components

Data access logic components provide simple access to database functionality (queries and data operations), returning both simple and complex data structures. They hide invocation and format idiosyncrasies of the data store from the business components and user interfaces that consume them. Implementing your data access logic in data access logic components allows you to encapsulate all the data access logic for the entire application in a single, central location, making the application easier to maintain or extend.

You should design each data access logic component to deal with only one data store. (This means that these components do not query and aggregate data from many sources; this is done by the business components.)

When using heterogeneous transactions, your data access logic components should participate in them, but they should never be the root of the transaction. It is more appropriate to have a business component as the root of a transaction in which one or more data access logic components are used to perform database updates.

Data Access Logic Component Functionality

When called, data access logic components typically do the following:

- Perform simple mappings and transformations of input and output arguments. This abstracts your business logic from database specific schemas and stored procedure signatures.

- Access data from only one data source. This improves maintainability by moving all data aggregation functionality to the business components, where data can be aggregated according to the specific business operation being performed.

- Act on a main table and perform operations on related tables as well. (Data access logic components should not necessarily encapsulate operations on just one table in an underlying data source.) This enhances the maintainability of the application.

Optionally, they may perform the following work:

- Use a custom utility component to manage and encapsulate optimistic locking schemes.

- Use a custom utility component to implement a data caching strategy for non-transactional query results.

- Implement dynamic data routing for very large scale systems that provide scalability by distributing data across multiple database servers.

Data access logic components should not:

- Invoke other data access logic components. Avoiding a design in which data access logic components invoke other data access logic components helps keep the path to data predictable, thus improving application maintainability.

- Initiate heterogeneous transactions. Since each data access logic component deals with only a single data source, there will be no scenario in which a data access logic component is the root for a heterogonous transaction. In some cases, however, a data access logic component may control a transaction that involves multiple updates in a single data source.

- Maintain state between method calls.

Data Access Logic Component Interface Design

Data access logic components commonly need to provide an interface to the following consumers:

- **Business components and workflows**. Data access logic components need to provide I/O of disconnected business documents and/or scalars in stateless, functional style methods, such as GetOrderHeader().

- **User interface components**. The user interaction components may use data access logic components for I/O of disconnected business documents for rendering data in rich clients and disconnected client scenarios, or for streaming output (for example, obtaining a DataReader) for ASP.NET and clients that benefit from stream rendering. You should consider using data access logic components directly from the user interface if you want to take advantage of the faster performance this design offers and you have no need for additional business logic between the user interface and data source.

Data access logic components may connect to the database directly using a data access API such as ADO.NET, or in more complex applications you may choose to provide an additional data access helper component that abstracts the complexities of accessing the database. In either case, you should strive to use stored procedures to perform the actual data retrieval or modification when using a relational database.

The methods exposed by a data access logic component may perform the following kinds of tasks:

- Common functionality that relates to managing "entities" such as CRUD functions.

- Queries that may involve getting data from many tables for read-only purposes. The data may be returned as paged or non-paged depending on your requirements, and the results may be streamed or non-streamed depending on whether the caller can benefit from it.

- Actions that will update data and potentially also return data.

- Returning metadata related to entity schema, query parameters, and resultset schemas.

- Paging for user interfaces that require subsets of data, such as when scrolling through an extensive product list.

Input parameters to data access logic component methods will typically include scalar values and business documents represented by XML strings or DataSets. Return values may be scalars, DataSets, DataReaders, XML strings, or some other data format. For specific design and implementation guidance in choosing a data format for your objects, see "Designing Data Tier Components and Passing Data Through Tiers" on MSDN (*http://msdn.microsoft.com/library/?url=/library/en-us/dnbda/html/BOAGag.asp?frame=true*).

Data Access Logic Component Example

The following C# code shows a partial skeleton outline of a simple data access logic component that could be used for accessing order data. This code is not intended to be a template for your code, but to illustrate some of the concepts from the discussion.

```csharp
public class OrderData
{
  private string conn_string;

  public OrderData()
  {
    // acquire the connection string from a secure or encrypted location
    // and assign to conn_string
  }
  public DataSet RetrieveOrders()
  {
```

```
    // Code to retrieve a DataSet containing Orders data
  }
  public OrderDataSet RetrieveOrder(Guid OrderId)
  {
    // Code to return a typed DataSet named OrderDataSet
    // representing a specific order.
    // (OrderDataSet will have a schema that has been defined in Visual Studio)
  }
  public void UpdateOrder(DataSet updatedOrder)
  {
    // code to update the database based on the properties
    // of the Order data sent in as a parameter of type dataset
  }
}
```

Recommendations for Data Access Logic Component Design

When designing data access logic components, you should consider the following general recommendations:

- Return only the data you need. This improves performance and enhances scalability.

- Use stored procedures to abstract data access from the underlying data schema. However, be careful not to overuse stored procedures, because doing so will severely impact the maintainability of your application in terms of code maintenance and reuse. A symptom of overusing stored procedures is having large trees of stored procedures that call each other. You should avoid using stored procedures to implement control flow, manipulate individual values (for example, perform string manipulation), or to implement any other functionality that is difficult to implement in Transact-SQL.

- Rely on RDBMS functionality for data-intensive work. Follow the principle, "Move the processing to the data, not the data to the processing." You should balance using stored procedures against the maintainability and reusability of your data logic.

- Implement a standard or expected set of stored procedures giving commonly used functionality, such as insert, read, update, and find functions. Doing so will save you time when you develop your business components. If you are proactive about implementing this functionality, you will be able to make the implementations consistent and enforce internal standards. If your design seems to be repeatable, you can even use code generators to build basic boilerplate stored procedures and data access logic component logic.

- Expose the expected functionality that is common across all your data access logic components in a separately defined interface or base class.

- Design consistent interfaces for different clients:
  - Your business components can be implemented in many ways, including the use of custom .NET code, BizTalk Orchestration rules, or a third-party business rule engine. The design of the interface for your data access logic components should be compatible with the implementation requirements of your current and potential business components to avoid having additional interfaces, façades, or mapping layers between both.
  - ASP.NET-based user interfaces will benefit in terms of performance from rendering data exposed as DataReaders. DataReaders are best for read-only, forward-only operations in which processing for each row is fast. If your data access logic components are deployed together with your user interface, you should expose large query results intended for rendering in data access logic component functions that return DataReaders. If you plan to operate on the data for a longer period of time, you can improve scalability by relying on a disconnected DataSet instead of a DataReader.

- Have the data access logic components expose metadata (for example, schema and column titles) for the data and operations it deals with. Doing so can help make applications more flexible at run-time, especially when rendering data in user interfaces.

- Do not necessarily build one data access logic component per table. You should design your data access logic components to represent a slightly higher level of abstraction and denormalization that is consumable from your business processes. It is uncommon to expose a relationship table as such; instead, you should expose the relationship functionality as data operations on the related data access logic components. For example, in a database where a many-to-many relationship between books and authors is facilitated by a TitleAuthor table, you would not create a data access logic component for TitleAuthor, but rather provide an AddBook method to an Author data access logic component or an AddAuthor method to a Book data access logic component. Semantically, you can add a book to an author or add an author to a book, but you cannot "insert authorship."

- If you store encrypted data, the data access logic components should perform the decryption (unless you want the encrypted data to go all the way to the client).

- If you are hosting your business components in Enterprise Services (COM+), you should build data access logic components as serviced components and deploy them in Enterprise Services as a library application. This allows them to participate and explicitly vote in Enterprise Services transactions and use role-based authorization. Data access logic components don't need to be hosted in Enterprise Services if you are not using any of the services or if they will be loaded in the same AppDomain as an Enterprise Services caller. For more information about using Enterprise Services, see "Business Components and Workflows" earlier in this chapter.

- Enable transactions only when you need them. Do not mark all data access logic components as *Require Transactions*, because this taxes resources and is unnecessary for read operations performed by the user interface. Instead, you should mark them as *Supports Transactions* by adding the following attribute:

```
[Transaction (TransactionOption.Supported)]
```

- Consider tuning isolation levels for queries of data. If you are building an application with high throughput requirements, special data operations may be performed at lower isolation levels than the rest of the transaction. Combining isolation levels can have a negative impact on data consistency, so you need to carefully analyze this option on a case-by-case basis. Transaction isolation levels should usually be set only at the transaction root (that is, the business process components). For more information, see Designing Business Layers earlier in this chapter.

- Use data access helper components. For benefits of this approach and details, see Designing Data Access Helper Components in this chapter.

For more information about designing data access logic components, see ".NET Data Access Architecture Guide" (*http://msdn.microsoft.com/library/default.asp?url= /library/en-us/dnbda/html/daag.asp*). Microsoft also provides the Data Access Application Block (*http://msdn.microsoft.com/library/en-us/dnbda/html/daab-rm.asp*), a tested, high-performance data helper component that you can use in your application.

Designing Data Access Helper Components

When an application requires large numbers of data access logic components to access the same data source, you may find that you need to implement similar generic data access code in each data access logic component. This duplication of logic can lead to maintainability issues and makes it difficult to troubleshoot data access problems. Centralizing generic data access functionality in a data access helper component can produce a cleaner, more manageable design. Data access helper components provide an easy invocation model to the underlying data source. You can consider data access helper components to be generic, caller-side façades into the data source. They are typically agnostic to the application business logic being performed. Usually you will only have one or two helper components for a given data source. Each one may implement different sets of technical functionality for accessing the service. For example, one data access helper component to a database may let you invoke stored procedures, while another one may allow you to stream large amounts of data out.

If you are designing your application to be agnostic to the data source type (for example, to be able to switch from an Oracle database to a SQL Server database), you can do so by having two simple data access helper components that expose a similar interface. Note, however, that changing the data source should warrant extra testing of your application and that "no touch" data source transparency is a dubious goal for most applications, possibly with the exception of "shrink wrapped" applications developed by ISVs.

The goal of using a data access helper component is to:

- Abstract the data access API programming model from the data-related business logic encapsulated in the data access logic components, thus reducing and simplifying the code in the data access logic components.
- Isolate connection management semantics.
- Isolate data source location (through connection string management).
- Isolate data source authentication.
- Isolate transaction enlistment (ADO.NET does this automatically when used to access data in a SQL Server database or when using ODBC or OLEDB).
- Centralize data access logic for easier maintenance, minimizing the need for data source-specific coding skills throughout the development team and making it easier to troubleshoot data access issues.
- Isolate data access API versioning dependencies from your data access logic components.
- Provide a single point of interception for data access monitoring and testing.
- Use code access and user-based or role-based authorization to restrict access to the whole data source.
- Translate non-.NET exceptions that may be returned by the data source into exceptions that your application can handle in traditional ways.

To see an example of a data access helper component, including source code and documentation, download the Data Access Application Block for .NET from MSDN (*http://msdn.microsoft.com/library/en-us/dnbda/html/daab-rm.asp*).

Accessing Multiple Data Sources

If you access an Oracle database or other data sources, you may prefer to abstract as much as possible the API with which you access them from your data access logic components. Microsoft has provided Oracle and OLE DB implementations of the Data Access Application Block and has stress-tested them in the context of the Nile performance benchmark. These implementations are available for download on MSDN by following the links in this article: *http://msdn.microsoft.com/library /default.asp?url=/library/en-us/dndotnet/html/manprooracperf.asp*.

Achieving RDBMS transparency is a complex design goal, and using data access helpers can help to mitigate some of the development, troubleshooting, and maintenance efforts. However, you will still need to test your application with each data source due to the different ways in which relational database management systems handle stored procedures, cursors, and other database artifacts.

If you are envisioning that your application may be deployed in different environments with different relational database management systems, you may want to implement your data access helpers with a common interface and provide the actual component that does the data access for a particular data source in a factory pattern. You can change the source code supplied for the Application Blocks for .NET mentioned earlier to accommodate these specific requirements.

Integrating with Services

If your business process involves external services, you will need to handle the semantics of communicating with each service you need to call. Specifically, you will need to use the correct communication API to call the service and perform any necessary translation between the data formats used by the service and those used by your business process. If the service contract consists of a long-running conversation, you will also need to keep intermediate state while waiting for a response.

You should use a service agent component that encapsulates the logic necessary to encapsulate these tasks and to initiate and manage a messaging-based conversation for each service your application must consume. You can think of service agents as data access logic components for services other than data stores, or as proxies or emissaries to other services. Some service publishers may provide callers with a ready-built service agent, while in other cases you may need to develop your own.

The goal of using a service agent is to:

- Encapsulate access to one service.
- Isolate the business process implementation from the service implementation in terms of data format or schema changes.
- Provide input and output data formats that are compatible with the business components calling the service.

Service agents may also perform the following common type of tasks if required:

- Perform basic validation of the data exchanged with the service.
- Cache data for common queries.
- Authorize access to the service, providing a granular way to check security before accessing the service from the calling application's perspective. Typically, the service will authenticate and authorize requests as well.
- Set the right security context or provide the right credentials to the service for authentication. For example, to set the credentials for an XML Web service you are invoking, you can use the HTTPCredentialCache.

- Make sure the right portions of the message are encrypted or that a secure channel can be established if necessary.

- Provide monitoring information that allows interaction with the service to be instrumented. This allows you to determine whether your partners are complying with their service level agreements (SLAs).

Managing Asynchronous Conversations with Services

In some cases, you will need to integrate your application with other services, both sending and receiving asynchronous calls. In this case, your service interfaces will be receiving calls from the outside services, and you will be making calls into those services from your service agents. If these message exchanges are implemented in an asynchronous way, you may need to keep track of the conversation a certain set of message exchanges belong to. You should use one of these two options to keep track of the conversation state:

- Use the business data in the messages to identify the conversation. For example, you could use an order ID number in all messages to identify the order you are processing in a particular message exchange. This is the most straightforward way of correlating messages.

- Provide an infrastructure component or utility that generates GUIDs or IDs for specific conversations and attaches them to messages. Your service agents and service interfaces will need access to this information to understand how to interpret a particular asynchronous call. You will also need a persistent database to track the state and ID of each conversation. This requires extra development, and the context of the message is lost if the message needs to be interpreted outside the service. However, it may be convenient to use your own correlation IDs if you want to maintain that information private.

For more information about this topic, see Chapter 3, "Security, Operational Management, and Communications Policies."

What's Next?

This chapter described recommendations for designing the different kinds of components that are common in distributed applications and services. Chapter 3, "Security, Operational Management, and Communications Policies" discusses the impact of organizational policies on the design of your application or service.

3

Security, Operational Management, and Communications Policies

Organizational policies define the rules that govern how an application is secured, how it is managed, and how the different components of the application communicate with one another and with external services. The policies affect the design of each layer of the application or service, as shown in Figure 3.1 on the next page.

Policies are not only determined at the organizational level, but they can be determined within organizations as well. It is useful in some cases to think of *zones*— all applications, services, or even application tiers are in the same zone if they share a subset of the policies. For example, an Internet-facing data center may have a different set of policies than the rest of a company's infrastructure, defining a special zone with tighter security restrictions than other parts of the application. Applications and services in this data center will thus be in a different zone than applications and services in the intranet. Understanding the policies of each component and thus defining the zones in which it will be executed is an important aspect of determining where to deploy components.

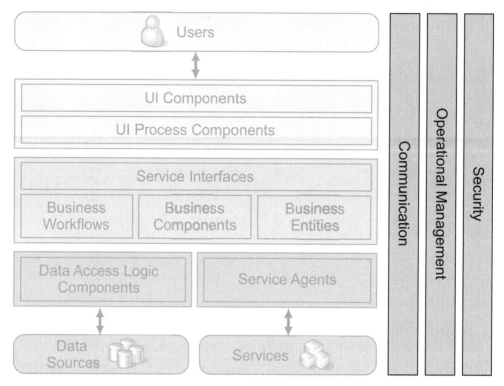

Figure 3.1
The effect of organizational policies on the application design

Chapter Contents

This chapter contains the following sections:

- Designing the Security Policy
- Designing the Operational Management Policy
- Designing the Communications Policy

Designing the Security Policy

The security policy is concerned with authentication, authorization, secure communication, auditing, and profile management, as shown in Figure 3.2.

Figure 3.2
Aspects of the security policy

General Security Principles

There are some general security principles that should be considered whenever you are designing a security policy. Consider the following guidelines:

- Whenever possible, you should rely on tested and proven security systems rather than building your own custom solution. Use industry-proven algorithms, techniques, platform-supplied infrastructure, and vendor-tested and supported technologies. If you decide to do custom development of security infrastructure, validate your approach and techniques with expert auditing and security review organizations before and after implementing it.

- Never trust external input. You should validate all data that is entered by users or submitted by other services.

- Assume that external systems are insecure. If your application receives unencrypted sensitive data from an external system, assume that the information is compromised.

- Apply the principle of least privilege. Don't enable more attributes on service accounts than those minimally needed by the application. Access resources with accounts that have the minimal permissions required.

- Reduce surface area. Risk will increase with the number of components and data you have exposed through the application, so you should expose only the functionality that you expect others to use.

- Default to a secure mode. Don't enable services, account rights, and technologies that you don't explicitly need. When you deploy the application on client and/or server computers, its default configuration should be secure.

- Don't rely on security by obscurity. Encrypting data implies having keys and a proven encryption algorithm. Secure data storage will prevent access under all circumstances. Mixing up strings, storing information in unexpected file paths, and so on, is not security.

- Follow STRIDE principles—STRIDE stands for Spoofing, Tampering, Repudiability, Information disclosure, Denial of service, and Elevation of privileges. These are classes of security vulnerabilities a system has to protect itself against. For more information about STRIDE, see "Designing for Securability" on MSDN at *http://msdn.microsoft.com/library/default.asp?url=/library/en-us/vsent7 /html/vxcondesigningforsecurability.asp.*

- "Check at the gate." Don't let processes progress any further than the first place at which you can authorize users.

- Lock your system down internally and externally: Internal users and operators may present at least as great a risk as external hackers.

Authentication

Authentication is defined as secure identification, which basically means that you have a mechanism for securely identifying your users that is appropriate for the security requirements of your application.

Authentication needs to be implemented in the user interface layer to provide authorization, auditing, and personalization capabilities. This usually involves requiring the user to enter credentials (such as a user name and password) to prove their identity. Other types of credentials include biometric readings, smartcards, physical keys, digital certificates, and so on.

If your application is exposed as a service, you will also want to authenticate on certain service interfaces to make sure that you are engaged in an exchange with a known and trusted partner, and that other external services don't spoof your application into believing it's somebody else who is calling.

Note: For more information about authenticating callers with Microsoft® ASP.NET, see "Authentication in ASP.NET: .NET Security Guidance" on MSDN (*http://msdn.microsoft.com/library/en-us /dnbda/html/authaspdotnet.asp*).

It is a goal of your design to have business logic that is transparent to the authentication process. For example, it is bad practice to have an extra parameter in component methods just to pass in user information, unless it is required by the business function.

Flowing Identity Across Tiers

The further a certain piece of functionality is from the user, the less meaningful the user identity becomes. In a services-based solution, some activities may not even be initiated by a user. You should have a design goal to reduce the relevance of the calling user the further an activity is from the user interface.

You may need to flow the identities of original callers (users or services) through your application layers to perform authorization or auditing. The identity may be that of an original caller (user or service) or a service account of an application tier. To flow the identity, you can let your communication mechanism flow the security context (for example, using Kerberos delegation with DCOM remoting), you can pass tokens or authentication tickets, or pass user ID or credentials.

Consider the following scenarios:

- The caller and the application being called do not share platform security subsystem or a common authentication mechanism. In this scenario, you aren't able to "flow" an existing security context; you need to reauthenticate by passing the appropriate credentials.

- The caller and the application being called are in trusted Microsoft Windows® domains, or the application performs authorization based on Windows identities or uses Microsoft .NET Enterprise Services roles. In this scenario, you need to choose a communication mechanism that flows Kerberos tickets or NTLM tokens. DCOM-RPC provides this capability. Using the information provided by the channel, you can recreate your custom principal and attach it to the thread based on the authentication information. Bear in mind that NTLM tokens can be used across only one network hop for authentication, and that Kerberos delegation requires policies at the computer, user, and domain levels. For more information, see "Designing the Communications Policy" later in this chapter or the following articles:

  - "Windows 2000 Kerberos Delegation" (*http://www.microsoft.com/technet /treeview/default.asp?url=/TechNet/prodtechnol/windows2000serv/deploy /kerberos.asp*)

  - "Impersonating and Reverting" (*http://msdn.microsoft.com/library /default.asp?url=/library/en-us/cpguide/html/cpconimpersonatingreverting.asp*)

- The caller and the application being called share a non-Windows authentication mechanism, such as a single sign-on solution or a centralized Web service that authenticates users. In this scenario, you flow tokens provided by the authentication service. You should pass these tokens in out-of-band mechanisms (not in function parameters) such as SOAP headers. The authentication mechanism should authenticate the user when presented with a valid token; this implies that the tokens it authenticates have no affinity with the originating computer. You must also make sure that the tokens can be authenticated in a time window large enough, especially for long-running transactions. Tokens are often produced with a hash of the user's credentials and a salt value. For the definition of salt value, see the Security Glossary on MSDN (*http://msdn.microsoft.com/library /default.asp?url=/library/en-us/security/Security/s_gly.asp*).

- The caller and the application being called are running in the same context. In this scenario, Microsoft .NET makes the call, keeping the existing CurrentPrincipal object on the thread. This is the case for all activities within the same AppDomain and for calling Enterprise Services–based applications with Library activation.

Authenticating with Other Services

Your application may need to invoke different services on behalf of a given user. Back-end single sign-on schemes map a given user's tokens and/or credentials for a set of services or data stores. For example, a user called "Bob" could be authenticated by your application and could access a legacy data store logging on as "Bobby." It is recommended that you design your application or service to access other data stores and other services using service accounts (for example, "SalesApplication") rather than impersonate the original user; however, stringent security requirements imposed by the organization may prevent this option. Development of account-mapping features can be complex, especially if you need to manage credentials, because, typically, user accounts must be kept synchronized. However, some account-mapping mechanisms, such as mapping client certificates to Windows accounts using Microsoft Internet Information Services (IIS), can be used very effectively.

If you need to impersonate user accounts in your own code, the current process needs to be able to call LogonUser, which on Windows 2000 requires the process user account have "act as part of the operating system" privileges. This is a very powerful privilege and it poses a serious risk if the process is compromised. It is not recommended that you use this privilege for the identities of applications based on ASP.NET or Enterprise Services except for very special cases.

Custom Authentication Mechanisms

You may need a custom authentication mechanism in your application if you have proven that you cannot leverage a platform-provided or third-party authentication mechanism. Using a custom authentication mechanism involves being able to store user accounts somewhere and have an algorithm to check whether supplied credentials are authenticated by the system. When implementing your own user authentication, consider the following guidelines:

- Implement the user authentication in a custom Identity object. You should have a constructor that takes user credentials and sets the internal flag for IIdentity.IsAuthenticated depending on the result. You can also have a constructor that takes an authentication token.

- Do not store user passwords. Instead, store a hash of the user's credentials plus salt values in the database. When authenticating, apply the same algorithm to the credentials supplied by the user—if the resulting string matches what you have stored in the database, the user has supplied the right credentials.

- Audit failed authentication attempts.

- Add a StrongNameIdentityPermission attribute to methods when you want to make sure that only your application assemblies can create and invoke your identity object.

- Expose the authentication token as a property of the Identity object. Your authentication token should be a hash involving the user name and other data. Include source data (such as computer name or calling assembly) if you want to restrict the token from being used elsewhere. To restrict the validity of your token to a certain span of time, you can add a timestamp to the hashed value. The complexity of the hash and encryption will depend on the risk of having the token compromised.

Authentication in the Presentation Layer

User interface components need to authenticate the user if the application needs to perform authorization, auditing, or personalization. A wide range of authentication mechanisms are available for Web-based user interfaces. To choose the right one for your scenario, see "Authentication in ASP.NET: .NET Security Guidance" on MSDN (*http://msdn.microsoft.com/library/en-us/dnbda/html/authaspdotnet.asp*). ASP.NET-based applications set the current principal in the OnAuthenticate event of Global.asax.

Windows-based user interfaces usually either rely on a custom authentication mechanism (where the application prompts for a user name and password), or they authenticate the user with their Windows logon. If you are using a custom authentication mechanism, you need to implement your own user interface to allow the user to log on, and set the correct Principal to the main thread and every thread the application creates.

User process components do not perform authentication; they rely on the security context set at application start as described earlier (for example, in the OnAuthenticate event of an ASP.NET-based application).

The user process components should run in the same user context as the user interface itself, so that all authentication tasks are delegated to the user interface or even the rendering infrastructure. For example, in ASP.NET any request to an ASPX page results in IIS requesting authentication credentials or ASP.NET redirecting the user to a forms-based authentication page. This is handled transparently to any user process layer and does not interrupt state flow, even when an authenticated session expires and needs to be reestablished.

Authentication in Business Components

The business components must authenticate the caller or delegate authentication to a service interface. The caller may be of many types, for example:

- A user interface component
- A user process component

- A business workflow (for example, a Microsoft BizTalk Server® XLANG schedule)
- Another business process component

The identity of the caller can be:

- A particular user.
- A service account representing the run-time identity of a particular portion of your application or an external system. For example, it could authenticate a call as coming from the Web UI tier.
- An external partner for which you have a special "service account."

If your business components authenticate callers, you need to consider how the three preceding caller identities can be authenticated and how they affect authorization.

Authentication in Data Access Components

Data access components are designed to be used by other components in the application or service. They are not usually intended for exposure for calling from scripts or other applications, so you can design them to rely on the security context set by the caller (the Principal object of the thread) or the authentication mechanism of your remoting strategy.

Data access components can authenticate with the database in two main ways:

- Using service accounts
- Impersonating the caller

In this case, you use one or a limited set of service accounts that represent roles or user type. In most cases, it will be just one service account, but you could use more if you need more fine-grained control over authorization. For example, in the order processing application you could access the database as "TheOrderApplication" or log on selectively as "OrderProcessingManager" or "OrderProcessingClerk" depending of the role of the caller identity.

Use service accounts when:

- You connect to the underlying data source from an environment in which impersonation of the initial caller is unavailable (for example, BizTalk Server).
- You have very limited change control over the accounts that can log on to the other system (for example, logging in to a relational database management system, which is strictly managed by the database administrator).
- The data store you are accessing has a different authentication mechanism than the rest of your application (for example, you are logging on to a Web service across the Internet).
- Accessing the data store through a large number of accounts negates connection pooling, thus degrading performance and scalability.

Do not use service accounts when:

- You don't have a secure way of storing and maintaining service credentials.
- You need to access the data store with specific user resources because of security policies (for example, you need access to data or objects in Microsoft SQL Server™ on behalf of users).
- The data store audits activities, and these audits need to map to individual users.

You are impersonating the caller when you access a data store with a set of accounts that map one to one with your application user base. For example, if "Joe" logs on to your application, and your data access components access a database, you are impersonating Joe if you log on to this database with Joe's credentials.

You need caller impersonation when:

- The data store performs authorization based on the logged on user.
- The data store needs to audit the activities of each individual end user.

Two implementation mechanisms are commonly used to impersonate callers:

- Platform impersonation services. Windows 2000 and later provides user impersonation through Kerberos across the network. This means that if Joe accesses your Web application, and you have used Windows authentication, you can impersonate Joe across the network all the way to your database.

  Impersonation is usually supported only if you have the same authentication mechanism all the way across the network, or a compatible standard authentication mechanism (such as Kerberos).

  In Windows 2000, the platform-provided impersonation level across multiple network hops is called *delegation.* To be able to delegate security context, the domain, computer, and user account need to be enabled for delegation. Windows .NET Server provides *constraint delegation*, which adds more management flexibility.

- Back-end single-sign-on solutions. Back-end single sign on mechanisms will provide you with the credentials (for example, user name and password) of a user to log on to a data source when you provide them evidence that you have authenticated that user by another mechanism. This type of approach is a form of "weak impersonation" because it requires a mapping that usually cannot propagate more than one logical hop.

For guidelines on connecting to SQL Server from your distributed applications, see the ".NET Data Access Architecture Guide" on MSDN (*http://msdn.microsoft.com /library/default.asp?url=/library/en-us/dnbda/html/daag.asp*).

Note: The considerations for implementing authentication in service agents are similar to those relating to data access components as described earlier.

Authentication in Business Entity Components

Business entity components are sometimes provided for custom development as an SDK or object model for the application to be used from script or the Microsoft Visual Basic® development system in clients.

If your business entities will not be used by other application components or custom script, they do not need to present an authentication boundary. In this case, they should rely on the current security context (the Principal object attached to the current thread) for authentication.

If you plan to expose business entities to allow custom scripting or consumption from other applications, you may need to provide an extra component that helps the client to "log on" from code and sets the security context required by these objects if you are not relying on platform authentication. You should not design business entities to rely on having a Windows security context for a particular human user if your business entities will be invoked by non-impersonating mechanisms (for example, a business process started asynchronously).

Authorization

The authorization aspect of the security policy is concerned with identifying the permissible actions for each authenticated security principal. In simple terms, the authorization policy determines who can do what. To determine your authorization policy, you need to take into account two major factors:

- User permissions and rights
- Code access security

User permissions and rights determine what a user account is permitted to do in the context of the application. Technically, the term "permissions" refers to allowable actions on a resource (such as a file or a database table), while "rights" refers to system tasks the user is allowed to perform (such as setting the system time or shutting down the computer). User permissions and rights can be assigned on an individual user-by-user basis, but are more manageable when users are arranged logically into groups or roles. Most resources have some kind of related permissions list, stating the permissions assigned to users for that particular resource. For example, in the Windows environment, resources are secured using an access control list (ACL), which lists the security principals assigned permissions on the resource, and what those permissions are. Permissions are usually cumulative, so a user who has "read" permission on a file and who is in a group that has "change" permission on the same file will have a net permission of "change." The exception to this rule is when a "deny" permission is assigned. If a user, or any of the groups that user is a member of, is explicitly denied access to a resource, the user cannot access the resource, regardless of any other user or group permissions that have been assigned.

Code access security, which was introduced by .NET, gives developers and administrators an extra dimension of access control and the possibility of cross-checking the correct security configuration. Unlike user permissions and rights, code access security is concerned with what an assembly can do. For example, a .NET assembly could be configured in such a way that the code is unable to access file system resources, and any code that attempts to do so will trigger an access violation exception. You can establish trust zones that apply different code access security policies to different assemblies based on a number of factors.

You need to incorporate the results in the following matrix into your access control design:

		User Access	
		Denied	Granted
Code Access	Denied	Denied	Denied
	Granted	Denied	Granted

User Access Security

User access security is used to determine what the current identity can do. You can check what a caller can do with many mechanisms. In applications with a user interface, your business logic may be impersonating the caller, but in most backends and especially services without user interfaces, your code will generally use as a specified "service" account.

Instead of using the actual account the current process is running as, you can set your own identity on a running thread manually by changing the Principal object.

What the user can do to the environment and platform is usually controlled with ACLs, which are checked against the current process or thread Windows identity. Common resources checked against the Windows identity are NTFS files, System APIs, .NET Enterprise Services (COM+) components, and services configured for Windows authentication.

Windows provides extensive group, user rights, and security management features. Some services may implement their own abstraction over these, such as role-based authorization in Enterprise Services. For example, Enterprise Services performs authorization against roles, where each role is actually an ACL.

.NET provides a comprehensive and extensible framework for managing user access security—including identities, permissions, and the notion of a principal and roles.

To make sure users in a certain role call into a given method, set an attribute on the class method, as shown in the following code.

```
[PrincipalPermission(SecurityAction.Demand, role="Managers")]
public void PlaceOrder(DataSet Order)
{
  // This code will not execute if the principal attached
  // to the thread returns false when IsInRole is invoked
  // with "Managers" as argument
}
```

For more information, see "PrincipalPermissionAttribute Constructor" in the .NET Framework SDK on MSDN (*http://msdn.microsoft.com/library/default.asp?url=/library/en-us/cpref/html/ frlrfsystemsecuritypermissionsprincipalpermissionattributeclassctortopic.asp?frame=true*).

If your component relies on being deployed in Enterprise Services and authenticates users through Windows, you can use Enterprise Services role management as shown in the following code.

```
[SecurityRole("HelpDesk")]
public DataSet GetCancelledOrders(System.Guid CustomerID)
{ //… }
```

If you are accessing your components remotely, the use of Enterprise Services role management requires you to access them through the DCOM-RPC channel.

Code Access Security

Code access security is concerned with what the assembly can do, but you can also decide whether your code runs or not, based on the code that is trying to access it. For example, this prevents your objects from being called from scripts that may be run unknowingly by someone with enough privileges. Note that code access security policy will not work through .NET remoting—all checks will be performed when invoked from the same application domain.

You can check code access based on the following factors:

- The application's installation directory
- The cryptographic hash of the assembly
- The digital signature of the assembly publisher
- The site from which the assembly originates
- The cryptographic strong name of the assembly
- The URL from which the assembly originates
- The zone from which the assembly originates

Security policies can be enforced for the enterprise, computer, user, and application. The zones defined by .NET are: Internet, intranet, MyComputer, NoZone, trusted, and untrusted. For in-depth information about these items, see the following articles in the MSDN Library:

- "Code Access Security" (*http://msdn.microsoft.com/library/default.asp?url=/library/ en-us/cpguide/html/cpconcodeaccesssecurity.asp*)

- "Introduction to Code Access Security" (*http://msdn.microsoft.com/library /default.asp?url=/library/en-us/cpguide/html/cpconintroductiontocodeaccesssecurity.asp*)

- "SecurityZone Enumeration" (*http://msdn.microsoft.com/library/default.asp?url= /library/en-us/cpref/html/frlrfsystemsecuritysecurityzoneclasstopic.asp*)

Implementing Complex Authorization Checks

In some cases, your application will need to perform complex authorization checks. For example, consider the following set of conditions: "Let this order placement go through if the caller is in the Salesman role, or if it is a service calling from a partner and the order does not exceed $1000, or if the caller is a Manager or a more powerful role." This authorization policy requires AND, OR, and "lesser than" and "greater than" combinations of permissions, plus knowledge about the price of the order being placed. These types of authorization checks are better performed in your own application code as programmatic checks, and require considerable development to separate them out as pure rules. In other, simpler scenarios, you can implement the authorization logic declaratively by using attributes or configuration settings.

Design of Custom Application-Level Authorization Schemes

Having a custom authorization scheme is a common requirement where a subset of the application authorization is managed by users and not operators, and authorization data is stored in your database or other external store. In these cases, your application will typically provide a user interface for security management and a database schema to manage role membership. When developing this type of framework, consider the following guidelines:

- Expose all your authorization logic through a principal object. Your principal will be created with a particular identity as a constructor argument. Check the IsAuthenticated property of the identity and use the name of your identity to locate the correct authorization data. Exposing your authorization logic through the IsInRole function lets your application use PrincipalPermission attributes and provides a consistent development model that lets you use other authentication and authorization schemes in the future. For an example of such a use, see "Creating WindowsIdentity and WindowsPrincipals Objects" on MSDN (*http://msdn.microsoft.com/library/default.asp?url=/library/en-us/cpguide/html /cpconcreatingwindowsidentitywindowsprincipalobjects.asp?frame=true*).

- Authenticate communication with the authorization data store. Make sure that the store of authorization data can't be compromised and that only the appropriate accounts can read and write this data. Your application should access this store with a read-only account, and only the parts of the application modifying this data should have read-write access.

- When not using Windows authentication, decouple user credentials and authentication identifiers from the authorization data schema. Your authorization data should refer internally to the users by a private ID. This lets you change authentication schemes in the future, lets your authorization rules be used from applications with different authentication mechanisms, and lets users change their user IDs.

- Cache for performance. You may decide to cache authorization information (for example, role membership) in your principal object instead of accessing the store every time. If you cache authorization data, you should sign or hash it to make sure it has not been tampered with.

- Provide offline capabilities for disconnected clients. This may involve embedding authorization logic with the client itself or caching a digitally signed copy locally.

- Design your authorization data store logic to be pluggable. This allows you to choose different locations and products without changing the framework design.

- Set code access calling assembly attributes with a StrongNameIdentityPermission attribute if you want to make sure that only your application assemblies can create and invoke your principal object.

Note: Windows .NET Server provides new features to help simplify the implementation of custom authorization functionality.

Users, Roles, and Trusted Applications and Services

Interacting applications and services usually have separate user accounts and role definitions, unless they are deployed in an organization where users and groups may be defined organization-wide. Even in this case, you should not rely on another service's definition of roles and users, but rather on your organization's role and user definitions and those defined for your service.

When dealing with interacting services, it is recommended that you authenticate and authorize callers at a service-wide granularity. For example, your service may interact with other services in partner organizations, in which case it will be useful to define roles such as "Standard Partner" and "Premier Partner." Using roles to perform authorization of external services and partners will enable your application to grow and work with many partners in the future without affecting your code or design.

If your service shares user accounts with calling services and needs to do authorization at the user granularity, user information should be contained as part of the exchanged business data. If you need to make sure that the business data was submitted by a particular user, you should include an authentication token or sign the document to show it came from the user or a service that you trust.

Setting Security Context at System Boundaries

A custom principal on a given thread doesn't flow across processes or through remoting channels, so you usually need to set the security system yourself at system boundaries.

To set a custom principal on the current thread you should:

1. Create the appropriate identity object, passing the credentials, user token, or user ID (or another type of identifier) into the constructor. If you have a custom implementation of the identity object, you will need to keep an internal flag indicating whether the identity has been authenticated.

2. Create your principal object, passing in the identity instance as an argument for the constructor. Your principal object should keep hold of this identity object so that it can return it when Iprincipal:Identity is called.

Windows principals flow with remoting if you are using DCOM-RPC as the remoting channel.

For more information about the .NET Principal and Identity objects and code samples illustrating this pattern for custom an windows principals, see "Principal and Identity Objects" on MSDN (*http://msdn.microsoft.com/library/default.asp?url= /library/en-us/cpguide/html/cpconprincipalidentityobjects.asp?frame=true*).

Authorization in User Interface Components

User interface components show data to users and gather data from them. Perform authorization at this level if you need to:

- Hide or show specific data fields to the user.
- Enable or disable controls for user input.

If the user is not supposed to see a certain piece of information, the most secure option is to avoid passing that piece of information to the presentation components in the first place.

It is common to perform some level of personalization of the root user interface or menu so that the user can only see the panes, Web parts, or menu entries that he or she can act on depending on his or her roles.

A user interface .exe file usually starts the application. You should set code access permissions on the user interface assemblies if you don't want to let it (or the local components it calls) access sensitive resources such as files.

You should consider the security context in which the presentation components of the application will run, and test them in an appropriately restricted environment.

Authorization in User Process Components

User process components manage data and control flow between user processes. You should perform authorization at this level if you need to:

- Control whether a user can start a user interface interaction process at all.
- Add and remove "steps" or full user interface components in a user interaction flow based on who is executing it. For example, a salesperson may see data for only his or her region, so there's no need to present him or her with a wizard step to choose the region of a sales report.

Ideally, the parent dialog box will be proactive and will hide or disable the user interface elements required to start a dialog box that a user is not authorized to use. If the parent dialog box is the "root" dialog box, then this means hiding the appropriate menu entries, dashboard Web parts, and so on, proactively.

You can set authorization declaratively for user processes by adding PrincipalPermission attributes to the classes or methods that implement them.

User process components are typically consumed only from user interface components. You can use code access security to restrict who is calling them. You can also use code access security to restrict how user process components interact with each other. This approach is especially important in portal scenarios where it is critical that a user process implemented as a plug-in cannot gather unauthorized information from other user processes and elements.

Authorization in Business Components

Take into account the following recommendations for authorization in business components:

- Try to make the business process authorization independent of user context, especially if you will use many communication mechanisms as queues and Web services, which won't let your process impersonate the caller.
- Use role-based security as much as possible rather than relying on user accounts. This provides better scalability, eases administration, and avoids problems with user names that support many canonical representations. You can define roles for serviced components in an Enterprise Services–based application, or you can use Windows groups or custom roles for .NET components that are not running in Enterprise Services.
- If you decorate a method with the PrincipalPermission attribute, always check the authentication type specified by the Identity object. The .NET PrincipalPermissionAttribute makes sure your principal is in a role, but does not specify an authentication mechanism.

Authorization in Service Agents and Service Interfaces

Service agents are the gateway through which calls to external services are made, so you should add authorization functionality to these components whenever you want to prevent specific users or roles from accessing them. Note that the external service may also implement its own further authorization checks.

You can implement authorization in service interface components using IIS and ASP.NET authentication for Web services, or using Windows ACLs if the service interface is exposed through Microsoft Message Queuing.

Authorization in Data Access Components

Data access components are the last components that expose business functionality before your application data, so they should perform any needed fine-grained authorization checks. Perform authorization at this level if you need to:

- Share the data access components with developers of business processes that you do not fully trust.
- Protect access to powerful functions exposed by the data stores.

Because data access components expose a fine-grained interface into the underlying systems, security can be managed only at a detailed level and does not take into account the aggregation needed for a particular business process operation. Thus, if you implement authorization checks at this level, granting or revoking permissions to execute a high-level business process to an identity may involve changing permissions for data access components as well.

To perform authorization, you can rely on Enterprise Services roles, and .NET PrincipalPermission attributes if you are using Windows authentication, or on .NET roles and attributes if you are not relying on a Windows security context.

If you are flowing the same user context into your data store, you can use the database's authorization functionality (for example, granting or revoking access to stored procedures). You can only do so if you are either:

- Using a set of service accounts to access the database representing different combinations of roles.
- Impersonating the callers all the way to your database.

Note: Flowing impersonated user contexts through to the database affects performance and scalability because connections are pooled per user. In addition, business processes started asynchronously will not automatically impersonate the originating user, and thus a Windows principal will be unavailable (unless you have access to the user's user name and password, which in most designs would be less secure and undesirable).

Because data access components are typically called only by other application components, they are a good candidate for restricting callers to the necessary set of assemblies—usually a combination of assemblies with components of the user interface layer, business process components, and business entities (if present).

Authorization in Business Entity Components

Business entity components can enforce authorization rules based on the security context of the caller (for both users and service accounts). For example, you can make sure that users in a particular role do not access private information of a Customer object. To implement this functionality, you will need to:

- Make sure that your security contexts are consistent in all physical tiers of your application: Different physical tiers that use business entities should have equivalent Principal objects in the running context.
- Place the appropriate checks through PrincipalPermission attributes and PrincipalPermision.Demand calls in your business entity calls.

You can enforce authorization on business entity components for proactive checks, but the final check should be performed by the business process components and data access components where the work is done. Note that having two places enforcing authorization over related functionality may entail more maintenance in keeping the authorization policies synchronized.

You may want to restrict access to business entity components from the code access standpoint. Doing so ensures that your business entities are invoked only by trusted code. You should do so to prevent power users from writing custom script against these objects to gain access to unauthorized information.

Secure Communication

In addition to authenticating users and authorizing requests, you must ensure that communication between the tiers of your application is secure to avoid attacks in which data is "sniffed" or tampered with while it is being transmitted or is being stored in a queue.

Secure communications involve securing data transfers between remote components and services.

Secure communication does not imply the use of an authentication mechanism, but may be coupled with the use of a one-way or two-way authentication mechanism that makes sure the communication endpoints are who they claim to be.

You have the following options for secure communications:

- Securing the whole channel:
  - Secure Sockets Layer (SSL). This is the recommended option for HTTP channels, is a widely accepted standard, and is usually accepted to open SSL ports on the firewalls. This option is recommended when exposing a service interface to the Web.
  - IPSec. This mechanism is a good choice when both endpoints of the communication are well known and are under your control. IPSec is used mostly when making calls between services or physical application tiers within a data center or across data centers of the same organization.
  - Custom remoting channel performing encryption. This approach is generally not recommended. Programming secure communications is a complex task that requires deep security skills and extensive testing.
  - Virtual private networks (VPNs). A VPN lets you establish a point-to-point IP transport over the Internet (or other networks). It is most suitable for providing a set of employees or partners access to an internal network from the Internet. Implementing VPN requires extensive infrastructure support.
- Securing the data:
  - Signing a message. This makes the message tamper-evident. Signatures can be used for authentication in the same process.
  - Encrypting a whole message. This makes the whole message unreadable if the network packets become compromised. Encrypting a message with the appropriate algorithms also make it tamper-evident.
  - Encrypting sensitive parts of the message. Use this when only a small part of the message is sensitive to being exposed.

Digital signing usually involves calculating a hash of the signed part of the message, encrypting the hash with the private key of the signer, and including the encrypted hash in the header. The receiver decrypts the signature received with the message using the public key of the signer, and it compares the resulting hash with the one it computes from the signed parts of the message. If the hashes match, it means that the message has not been tampered with. If they don't match, the message has been corrupted and you should audit the failed message and caller information and return an exception.

Note: Digitally signed and hashed messages can still be used in a replay attack, in which the same message is sent repeatedly to the server. You may need to build further mitigation logic into your messaging layer to deal with this kind of attack. For example, you could add a timestamp to the message body or design your process so that messages are idempotent.

For example, with XML Web services, you can implement XML digital signatures in SOAP by using the SignedXml class and SOAP headers. For more information about the SignedXml class, see "SignedXml Class" on MSDN (*http:// msdn.microsoft.com/library/default.asp?url=/library/en-us/cpref/html/ frlrfSystemSecurityCryptographyXmlSignedXmlClassTopic.asp*). For more information about SOAP headers, see "Using SOAP Headers" on MSDN (*http:// msdn.microsoft.com/library/default.asp?url=/library/en-us/cpguide/html/ cpconusingsoapheaders.asp?frame=true*).

Securing the communication channel will affect performance, so whenever you are evaluating the techniques described earlier, you should scope the channel security to those specific areas where it is needed, such as securing specific Web service URIs, specific ASP.NET pages, or sensitive pieces of business data. Different mechanisms will have different performance implications depending on what data your application exchanges, the number of endpoints, and the type of security required.

For more information about channels that support secure communication channels, see "Designing the Communications Policy" later in this chapter.

Secure Communication in User Interface Components

User interface components communicate only with the user. In general, you should avoid showing sensitive information without a warning. Passwords should never be displayed or transmitted in plain text. For Web applications, you should use SSL whenever sensitive data is being exchanged with the user, such as when submitting logon forms or displaying personal financial information.

User process components typically reside together with the user interface components, so there is no need to secure the channel between them.

Secure Communication in Service Agents and Service Interfaces

It is the role of the service agent to establish the appropriate channel security mechanism between itself and the invoked service. For example, if messages need to be signed or if an SSL connection is needed, the service agent must implement this logic to isolate these requirements from the business components and workflows.

A service interface such as an XML Web service may need to enforce the need for secure communications, repudiating connections and messages that do not comply. Both Message Queuing and XML Web services make it easy to establish a secure communication channel. For more information, see "Designing the Communications Policy" later in this chapter.

Secure Communication in Data Access Components

Data access components typically rely on data access helper components to perform the connections with the data store. It's these components that should handle any kind of communication encryption policy with the data store. Additionally, specific data stores may support multiple communications protocols (for example, SQL Server supports named pipes, TCP/IP, IPX/SPX, and others). The communications policy of the organization could affect this aspect of the design by dictating a particular protocol.

Different data sources support different types of communication security, or may even support none natively. Sometimes you will need to protect communication with the service with a platform-provided or standard security mechanism, such as SSL.

Data access helper components should manage the connection parameters to enforce communication security. For example, data access helper components can encapsulate the following:

- Logic to choose the appropriate security provider for SQL Server
- Implementation of SOAP encryption mechanisms
- Code to establish a connection over SSL

Profile Management

User profiles consist of information about the user that your application can use to customize its behavior. A user profile may include user interface preferences (for example, background colors) and data about the user (for example, the region he or she is in, credit card details, and so on). Profile information can be exposed as a collection by the Principal object. You may decide to cache profile information for offline applications. If the profile information contains sensitive data, you may consider encrypting it or hashing it to make sure that it can't be read and that it hasn't been tampered with.

Auditing

In many cases, you will need to implement auditing functionality to track user and business activity in the application for security purposes. To audit your business activities, you need a secure storage location—in fact, auditing can be thought of as "secure logging." If you are implementing your own auditing solution, you must make sure that audit entries are tamper-proof or at least tamper-evident (achieved with digital signatures) and that storage location is secured (for example, connection strings cannot be changed and/or storage files cannot be replaced). Your auditing mechanism can use document signing, platform authentication, and code-access security to make sure that spurious entries cannot be logged by malicious code.

The auditing interface to your application may be exposed as a utility function or as a method of the application's Principal object if the audited action needs to be correlated with the user.

Auditing in User Interface and User Process Components

The activity that occurs in the user interface components is not usually audited. A user interface application may want to audit global events such as logon, logoff, password changes, and all security exceptions in general.

Because user process components represent user activities (that may be stopped, abandoned, and so on) it is not common to audit them. As always, you may want to audit security-related exceptions.

Auditing in Business Process Components

Business processes are prime auditing targets. You will want to know who performed key business activities and when the activities occurred.

If you are auditing within the context of a transaction, to a transactional resource manager such as SQL Server, you will want to have a new transaction started by your auditing component, so failures in the original transaction tree don't also roll back the audit entry.

Auditing in Data Access Components

Data access components are the closest custom business logic layer to the data store. Just as it is for fine-grained authorization, the data access components layer is a good location for implementing fine-grained auditing.

Your data access components will usually invoke stored procedures that actually do the data-intensive work, so you may want to also audit inside the RDBMS. For information about how to implement auditing in SQL Server, see "Auditing SQL Server Activity" in the SQL Server 2000 SDK on MSDN (*http://msdn.microsoft.com /library/default.asp?url=/library/en-us/adminsql/ad_security_2ard.asp*).

Designing the Operational Management Policy

The operational management policy is concerned with the ongoing, day-to-day running of the application, and covers issues such as exception management, monitoring, business monitoring, metadata, configuration, and service location, as shown in Figure 3.3.

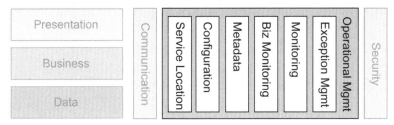

Figure 3.3
Aspects of the operational management policy

Exception Management

Exception management encompasses catching and throwing exceptions, designing exceptions, flowing exception information, and publishing exception information to diverse users.

All applications should implement some kind of exception handling to catch run-time errors. Exceptions should be caught and resolved if possible. If an error state cannot be resolved, the application should display a meaningful message to the user and provide some way of logging or publishing the exception information for debugging purposes.

Note: For more information about handling exceptions in .NET-based applications, see "Exception Management in .NET" on MSDN (*http://msdn.microsoft.com/library/default.asp?url= /library/en-us/dnbda/html/exceptdotnet.asp*).

For a Microsoft-provided reference building block for exception management that implements the outlined design, see "Exception Management Application Block for .NET" on MSDN (*http://msdn.microsoft.com/library/default.asp?url=/library/en-us /dnbda/html/emab-rm.asp*).

Catching and Throwing Exceptions

Your code should catch exceptions if it is capable of adding relevancy to the exception information or making a business flow decision based on the type and data of the exception. It is advisable to catch exceptions at layer boundaries in order to wrap them in exception types that are relevant to the callers. You can throw a new exception, and optionally preserve the original caught exception as an InnerException member of the new exception object you are throwing.

Designing Exception Classes

Exceptions classes for your application should derive from ApplicationException. You may decide to build your own exception class that provides more features, such as the ability to add arbitrary data to the exception. The Exception Management

Application Block for .NET provides a base class that you can use to derive from that provides these extra features.

It is common to derive two main branches of exceptions: business exceptions and technical exceptions. This design makes it easier to catch and publish the appropriate type of exceptions in different parts of your application.

Flowing Exception Information

Exceptions provide an upstream information flow. Exceptions need to be serializable in order to flow upstream across tiers. This is especially important when reaching a service interface or user interface that you don't want to flow the exception verbatim, but rather translate it into something actionable for the caller, and without exposing sensitive business or technical information about your application and service (such as a database connection string in case of a connection failure) that could be used against the system or organization.

Exceptions will flow only if the communication is two-way. In the case of Message Queuing and one-way communication mechanisms, you will need to implement your own mechanism to let the caller know that the message caused an error. The client also needs to be able to handle failures that prevent messages from reaching the server at all.

Publishing Exception Information

If an exception occurs, you want your application to notify the appropriate people. Operations and technical support staff need to know about technical exceptions, and managers and helpdesk users may need to know about business exceptions. Each type of audience will want additional environment information about the exception to perform its role, such as OrderIDs or source computers.

You should publish relevant information for each audience through channels that communicate with the tools used by them. This means that your application may publish some Windows Management Instrumentation WMI events in case of a technical exception, contact a helpdesk Web service in case of a business exception, and log exceptions to the event log in all cases.

For tested code that implements these features, see the "Exception Management Application Block for .NET" on MSDN (*http://msdn.microsoft.com/library/ default.asp?url=/library/en-us/dnbda/html/emab-rm.asp?frame=true*).

Exception Management in User Interface Components

User process components will need to handle exceptions coming from the business processes and data access components, and decide whether to:

- Retry the operation.
- Expose the issue to the user.
- Stop, restart, or continue with the user interface flow of the application.

User process components may need to hide exceptions from the user, depending on the operation. If the exception needs to be displayed, the user process will probably branch control execution to some visual representation of the error, and not propagate it to its caller (which may be an ASP.NET page or Windows form, for example).

ASP.NET provides some basic error-state user interface flow capabilities which you may leverage in such applications. For more information, see "Exception Management in .NET" on MSDN (*http://msdn.microsoft.com/library/en-us/dnbda/html/exceptdotnet.asp*).

User interface components should publish their exceptions to help isolate problems, especially in rich client applications. It is common to publish the exceptions to some central server (for example, through Web services) and/or to a local file or event log in the case of disconnected applications.

Exception Management in Business Process Components

Handling exceptions in the business components often requires catching exceptions and errors returned by the business objects and abstracting them into an exception that can be understood by the caller. Business components need to handle exceptions coming from the data access components. These include:

- Technical exceptions (for example, a failed database connection).
- Business exceptions (for example, violation of a foreign key constraint).

The business components should not hide these exceptions from the calling code and should propagate the exceptions they receive. Microsoft recommends propagating the exceptions as they are, but you may choose to wrap them, especially if you have only one type of client that may benefit from higher-level exception information.

Business components should raise new exceptions when:

- The caller is trying to perform an operation with insufficient or incorrect data (for example, calling the Save method on a Customer object for which no first name has been provided).
- A constraint violation occurs when performing an operation.

Business components need to propagate all data access components exceptions; for example, if:

- There are technical problems accessing the data or errors raised from the back-end data access components. Most of these exceptions can be propagated without rewrapping.
- You are using an optimistic locking scheme (this is common when the business entities are used from the user interface layers) and an update would overwrite data that has been updated since it was read.

In general, business components should not hide any exception raised from the layers they call. Hiding exceptions could mislead business processes in terms of transactional state and make the user believe that certain operations were successful.

Exceptions should be published in business layers, because this is where transaction outcome is known and internal service level agreements are defined.

Exception Management in Data Access Components

Data access components will usually need to handle two main classes of exceptions:

- Exceptions deriving from technical errors connecting to and invoking the data store.
- Business exceptions deriving from stored procedures implementing data-intensive business logic.

If the running activities are transactional, all exceptions will abort the current transaction. It is important that your data access components explicitly vote on the current Enterprise Services transaction if something has gone wrong.

Handling exceptions in the data components often requires catching exceptions and errors returned by the underlying data source (or data access API) and mapping them to the exception schema used in the rest of the application. Data access components should propagate exceptions, wrapping them in exception types that make sense for their clients. Wrapping the exceptions in two main exception types (business and technical) improves exception handling structure and exception publishing logic for the potentially diverse callers.

The functionality to map data source exceptions (for example, SqlExceptions, which represent SQL Server errors raised with RAISERROR in stored procedures) to your .NET-based application exception schema should be implemented in the data access components. Performing the mapping may involve one or more of the following:

- Translating or mapping a service-specific error code or HResult into an exception of the appropriate type in .NET.
- Wrapping a low-level .NET exception with a more significant exception.
- Extracting verbose error information through the service API and adding the information to the appropriate fields of the exception being created.

Note: If the data access API is designed for .NET (as ADO.NET is), most of this translation and wrapping is done automatically, so catching and re-throwing is unnecessary in the data access components. ADO.NET, for example, throws a SqlException exception when an error is returned by SQL Server. However, in most cases, you should wrap these data access API–specific exceptions in custom exceptions that have more relevance in your application.

Data access components should always publish their exceptions by writing exception details to a log file, sending an alert, or otherwise publishing the exception. Technical exceptions and business exceptions may be published using different mechanisms (for example you might choose to send alerts to operators through WMI when a technical issue arises, but log business exceptions to an application-specific error log or database).

Exception Management in Business Entity Components

Business entities may be called from the user interface or business process components, so it's important that you raise and propagate exceptions that can be consumed by both.

In the special cases where your business entities are exposed for consumption by script developers as an SDK to a larger system, you may choose to wrap all exceptions in friendlier exception types that contain the original exception as an InnerException member.

Monitoring

You need to instrument your application to give your operations staff insight into application health, compliance with service level agreements (SLAs), and scaling/capacity management. For detailed guidelines on how to add instrumentation to your application, see "Monitoring in .NET Distributed Application Design" on MSDN (*http://msdn.microsoft.com/library/default.asp?url=/library/en-us/dnbda/html/monitordotnet.asp?frame=true*).

Your application may benefit from the following types of monitoring:

- Health monitoring: Are the components running well? Are there transient locks, hangs, process exits, blocked queues and so on?
- SLA compliance: Are the business processes running within the expected parameters? Are the services you integrate with meeting expectations? Is your application or service meeting your caller's performance and turnaround expectations?
- Scale management: Is the computer, farm, or network that the components are deployed within correctly designed for the task they are handling? Is performance predictable from available resources?
- Business monitoring: Can you make your business processes more efficient? Can critical decisions be made earlier? What are the organizational bottlenecks to efficient business processing?

These different questions can be answered by monitoring the right parts of your application or service. Not all types of monitoring need to be active at all times. For example, you may decide to monitor business factors before planning the next version of your application.

Business Monitoring

Business monitoring is intended to provide a reactive capacity to business decision makers with regard to business process health, business-level SLA compliance, and organizational capacity management. Rather than telling you there are network errors, this type of monitoring gives you an insight into business structure and process efficiency. For example, you may determine that business processes are stalled for days whenever a certain partner is involved in shipping and handling.

Business monitoring is a component of business intelligence, but does not replace other techniques such as OLAP analysis and data mining, which derive their data from ETL (extract, transform, load) processes from the application or service's stores to inform proactive decisions based on trends of past data. The main distinguishing factor is that business metrics are transient and may not even be reflected in the application data.

Monitoring in User Process Components

User process components may provide interesting business statistics to improve application UI design and efficiently interact with users. The following are some examples of indicators you can obtain from user process components:

- Average total duration for a given user process.

- Whether user processes tend to pause at a certain point, typically indicating that the user interface could provide more complete business information or could be more self-explanatory.

- What user processes are started and never finished, and at what stage they are dropped off in an incomplete state. You may be able to use this information to design user interfaces that let a user decide whether to start the process at all in an earlier stage.

Monitoring in Business Process Components and Workflows

Health monitoring of your business components and workflows is critical, because it is where transaction outcome is ultimately known, and where compensation, service, and data store problems are channeled. You should instrument your classes as described in "Monitoring in .NET Distributed Application Design" on MSDN (*http://msdn.microsoft.com/library/default.asp?url=/library/en-us/dnbda/html/monitordotnet.asp?frame=true*).

Most (if not all) business-level monitoring is typically done in the business layers. If your business layers are implemented with Enterprise Services (COM+), you can use AppMetrics for COM+ from XTremesoft (*http://www.xtremesoft.com/*). For BizTalk workflow monitoring, you can use BizTalk Document Tracking. XTremesoft also provides a product called AppMetrics for BizTalk Server.

For more information about tracking documents in BizTalk Server, see "Using BizTalk Document Tracking" on MSDN (*http://msdn.microsoft.com/library /default.asp?url=/library/en-us/biztalks/htm/lat_track_docs_gsra.asp*).

Monitoring in Data Access Components

Data access components participate in transactions and talk to data access API components that handle connection with data services. These components are important candidates for monitoring in order to track the duration of long-running data operations, object lifetime duration, activity throughput and latency, memory usage, and other technical indicators of health.

Transactional aborts are expensive to the application as a whole. Monitoring these components and having a good exception publishing policy will help you isolate components that tend to fail from a business logic or technical perspective.

Whenever you are connecting to a database, you should also monitor connection usage, connection pooling statistics, and connection security statistics.

It is also common to monitor the response time of the external data if an SLA is associated with the use of the data or external data source.

For guidelines on how to add monitoring capabilities to your components, see "Monitoring in .NET Distributed Application Design" on MSDN (*http:// msdn.microsoft.com/library/default.asp?url=/library/en-us/dnbda/html /monitordotnet.asp?frame=true*).

If your business layers are implemented with Enterprise Services, you can use AppMetrics for COM+ from XTremesoft, or use instrumented classes as described in "Monitoring in .NET Distributed Application Design."

Configuration

Applications require configuration data to function technically. Settings that modify the behavior of the policies (security, operational management, and communications) are considered configuration data.

Configuration data is maintained in .NET configuration files at the user, machine, and application level. Custom configuration stored here can be defined with any schema and can be accessed easily by using the ConfigurationSettings class in your application.

It is very important to consider configuration security sensitivity—for example, you should not store SQL connection strings in clear text in XML configuration files, especially if they contain SQL credentials. You should restrict access to security information to the proper operators, and for added security, you may consider digitally signing information to make sure that the configuration data has not been tampered with.

Configuration data can be stored in many places, each one with its advantages and disadvantages:

- Application XML configuration files: Storing configuration data here enables your application clients to work offline, and this model is easy to implement. With rich client applications, this approach may increase change management costs because it requires that all your clients have the same configuration information. In server environments, it is easy to push configuration changes using Application Center server or Microsoft Active Directory directory services, or by copying batch files. Note that reloading application configuration data requires an AppDomain restart. However, ASP.NET will restart the AppDomain for you when it detects a change in the configuration files. Application configuration files are stored in plain text, which may be an unacceptable security risk. For example, in most scenarios you should not store connection strings containing user names and passwords in application configuration files.

- SQL Server or the application data store: This is a common storage location for application-managed configuration data, but even more so for application metadata. If you store configuration here, it is recommended that you keep your metadata in a different SQL Server database than your business data. Accessing the database often results in a performance hit, so you should consider caching.

- Active Directory: Within an organization, you may decide to store application metadata in Active Directory. Doing so makes the metadata available for clients on the domain. You can also secure the information in Active Directory with Windows ACLs, making sure that only authorized users and service accounts can access it.

- Constructor strings: If you are using Enterprise Services–based components, you can add configuration data to the constructor string for the components.

- Other locations for special cases: These include the Windows Registry, the Windows Local Security Authority (LSA) store, and custom implementations. They are used in very special cases and add requirements for the application privileges on the machine and deployment mechanisms.

- Third-party configuration management solutions that may also provide versioning and deployment features.

Accessing configuration data and metadata frequently can cause a performance hit, especially if the data is stored remotely. To prevent this, you can cache application-managed configuration data and metadata in memory. However, you need to make sure that you are not adding a security hole by exposing sensitive information to the wrong application code. If you cache configuration data, it is useful to specify refresh rates and frequencies so that the cached data is flushed and refreshed at predetermined times rather than at relative intervals (for example, force configuration cache refreshes every hour on the hour, not "one hour since the last refresh").

This helps your operators understand what configuration data your application is based on at a given point in time.

Configuration in the Presentation Layers

Your user process components usually require the following configuration settings:

- Location information to reach the business process components and the data access components.
- Connection data (such as a connection string or a file path) for the resource that handles persisting user process data for long-running processes.

Configuration in Service Agents

Service agents need to have configuration information to connect to the external service using Web services, message queuing, or some other means. The configuration schema and data depends on the particular service being accessed.

Configuration in Data Access Components

Your data access components usually need the following:

- They need to have the ability to map logical data source names to physical connection parameters (for example, to map the "Sales" database to an actual connection string).
- If your data access components perform dynamic data routing, you will need to have configuration data that expresses the routing parameters (for example, customer region), algorithms (for example, hashing), and routing destinations (for example, connection strings for databases). It is common to wrap dynamic data routing logic in a separate utility component.

Metadata

To make your application more flexible with regard to changing run-time conditions, you may want to provide it with information about itself. Designing your application to use metadata in certain places can make it easier to maintain and enables it to adapt to change without costly redevelopment or deployment.

There are two main times when you can use metadata in your application:

- **Design time.** For example, you may use information about your database to generate code, stored procedures, .NET classes, or even user interface components for commonly repeated patterns. Using metadata during development saves reactive development time, reduces the need for communication between teams, concentrates and "persists" special skill sets, and enforces design, naming, and implementation standards. The resulting components behave more predictably and are less prone to errors, so developer productivity increases. However, this approach requires specialized knowledge and an initial extra development effort in creating the templates and the code that combines them with the metadata.

- **Run time.** Your application may be easier to maintain if you take advantage of the right metadata for commonly changing aspects. For example, you may decide to take headers for a UI list or grid from metadata, so they are not hardcoded into your application. Your application may also take advantage of metadata when establishing relationships between components or when processing predictable patterns, such as validation rules. However, using metadata at run time is usually expensive in terms of performance, so you should test and profile your application design early in the application lifecycle. You can design your components to expose metadata about themselves, but you should do so only if your application plans to use it; otherwise, the metadata could be a security hole.

You can avoid performance issues when using metadata at run time by using advanced techniques such as generating code on the fly and compiling it using the .NET reflection classes *while the application is running*. This design technique is complex and is not recommended for any but the most complex scenarios due to the skills required and the security implications of run-time code compilation and metadata storage. Run-time customization can be more easily achieved in most cases with .NET scripting. For more information about .NET scripting, see "Script Happens .NET" on MSDN (*http://msdn.microsoft.com/library/default.asp?url=/library /en-us/dnclinic/html/scripting06112001.asp?frame=true*).

Metadata can be stored in multiple places as discussed earlier in "Configuration." For centralized stores, you can use SQL Server databases or Active Directory. If you want to distribute your metadata alongside your assemblies, you can implement it in XML files, or even custom .NET attributes.

For a good conceptual foundation on the use of metadata in software design (a technique sometimes called metaprogramming, which is related to intention-based programming) read *Generative Programming: Methods, Tools and Applications* by Krzysztof Czarnecki and Ulrich Eisenecker (ISBN: 0201309777).

The following discussion illustrates potential uses of metadata.

Metadata in User Interface Components

You usually use metadata in user interfaces to specify column headers, user assistance text, error messages, menu hierarchies, and other types of information that do not ultimately affect the business data of your application.

If your application requires some level of customization, it is common to use metadata to manage simple customization options. For more complex customizations, it is better to use .NET scripting.

Metadata in User Process Components

If you model your user processes in a consistent way, you may find that having the following metadata helps you create a more maintainable design:

- What user processes exist and what menu items trigger them
- What internal business state is needed for the UI process, and what the default values are.
- A representation of the behavior of the user process, such as what UI component to show when the customer clicks "Confirm purchase."

Metadata in Business Components

Your business processes may benefit from using metadata to model simple rules or patterns. For example, a pipeline pattern may be implemented as an engine that uses metadata to determine what classes and methods to call in what sequence, as illustrated by the Microsoft Commerce Server 2002 purchasing pipelines. You may also use metadata to help calling components identify compensation methods for particular business activities.

Metadata in Data Access Components

If your data access component exposes an interface that provides Create, Read, Update, and Delete (CRUD) functionality, it could be useful to expose the schema of the returned data and metadata it uses. Similarly, it is useful to expose XSD schemas of complex input and output parameters for special queries or actions.

Your data access components may rely on metadata instead of procedural code to perform data transformations and mapping. You can use XSL documents to transform one XML schema into another, use a rules-based approach to do the mapping, or use SQLXML annotated schemas to map XML documents to data in the underlying database. Using a metadata-based approach may be especially useful if this mapping tends to change often.

Metadata in Business Entity Components

It is recommended that you expose business entity metadata to consumers, especially to user interface components, where it is helpful to have information about the business entities available to assist in such tasks as:

- Filling column headers in tables.
- Displaying descriptions of attributes for tooltips and user interface friendliness.
- Using relationships between logical entities in your application to let the user interface expose them and allow their navigation.
- Validating business entity data values, so the user interface can proactively enforce them (for example, the maximum number of addresses per customer, or data formats).

You can expose metadata in form of XSD or XML documents with a custom schema.

It is also recommended that you keep frequently changing validation rules as metadata. Designing your validation rules as metadata enables you to change them without affecting the implementation or redeploying the business entity components. This is particularly important because business entities may be used from client desktops where change management is expensive. Validation rules for entities could be expressed in an XSD schema deployed with the application.

Service Location

When calling remote services, you need to determine where .NET objects and external services that can process your request are located and how to reach them. This is especially important when you are using Web services hosted by other organizations or third parties.

Locating Local Assemblies

.NET provides extensive features to let you specify what assemblies to link to at run time. For in-depth technical information on how .NET locates local assemblies when creating objects, see "How the Runtime Locates Assemblies" on MSDN (*http:// msdn.microsoft.com/library/default.asp?url=/library/en-us/cpguide/html /cpconhowruntimelocatesassemblies.asp*).

Locating Classes for .NET Remoting

.NET remoting enables you to call objects located in another application domain, process, or computer. You can expose objects to be used by remoting, and locate objects you want to call remotely, by specifying configuration information or by writing code in your application. You will also need to let your application know about the channels you intend to use for remote communication.

For more information about using .NET remoting configuration to expose types, find types, and register channels, see "Registering Remote Objects Using Configuration Files" on MSDN (*http://msdn.microsoft.com/library/default.asp?url=/library/en-us /cpguide/html/cpconregisteringremoteobjectsusingconfigurationfiles.asp?frame=true*).

Locating Message Queuing Queues for Asynchronous Messaging

To send a Message Queuing message, you need to know which queue you are sending it to. The way you reference Message Queuing queues varies depending on Message Queuing configuration and whether you are sending messages over the Internet.

If Message Queuing has been installed in domain configuration, you can locate queues by name, ID, or other attributes. With MSMQ 2.0 (found in Windows 2000), this capability requires that your queue clients and servers refer to the same domain controller that maintains a registry of existing queues in Active Directory. In domain configurations, you can specify a label or FormatName to identify the queue.

If you installed Message Queuing in a workgroup configuration on the sender, you need to specify the full path of the queue. For more information about using Message Queuing, see the following MSDN articles:

- "MessageQueue.Path Property" (*http://msdn.microsoft.com/library/default.asp?url= /library/en-us/cpref/html/ frlrfSystemMessagingMessageQueueClassPathTopic.asp?frame=true*)

- "MessageQueue.QueueName Property" (*http://msdn.microsoft.com/library/en-us /cpref/html/frlrfsystemmessagingmessagequeueclassqueuenametopic.asp*)

Locating Web Services on the Internet and Within an Organization

The URI for an XML Web service can be retrieved dynamically at run time from the application configuration file. This approach enhances your application's maintainability. For more information about storing Web service location information in the configuration file, see "Web References" on MSDN (*http://msdn.microsoft.com/library /default.asp?url=/library/en-us/vsintro7/html/vxconWebReferences.asp?frame=true*).

An industry initiative called UDDI (Universal Description, Discovery, and Integration) exists to help services and businesses find other services and expose services and their interfaces to interested callers. UDDI is based on standards such as SOAP, WSDL, and DNS, which makes it inherently platform-independent. You can use a worldwide UDDI registry to expose your service to the outside partners and services. Additionally, you can deploy an implementation of the UDDI specification in your enterprise to help locate and integrate internal services.

Microsoft provides UDDI Services natively with Microsoft Windows .NET Server. For more information about this feature, see the Windows .NET Server Web site (*http://www.microsoft.com/windows.netserver/developers/default.mspx*). If you do not have Microsoft .NET Server, you can also use the Microsoft UDDI SDK (*http:// www.microsoft.com/downloads/release.asp?ReleaseID=35940*) to install UDDI on a local computer.

For more information about UDDI, see the UDDI Web site (*http://www.uddi.org/*) and the following MSDN articles:

- "UDDI – an XML Web Service" (*http://msdn.microsoft.com/library/default.asp?url= /library/en-us/dnexxml/html/xml12182000.asp?frame=true*)

- "Using UDDI at Run Time" (*http://msdn.microsoft.com/library/default.asp?url= /library/en-us/dnuddi/html/runtimeuddi1.asp?frame=true*)

Designing the Communications Policy

The communications policy defines how the components in your application will communicate with each other. The communications policy covers such issues such communication synchronicity, format, and protocol, as shown in Figure 3.4.

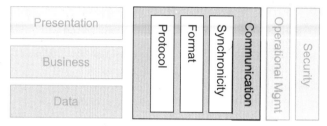

Figure 3.4
Aspects of the communications policy

Choosing the Correct Communication Model

You should carefully consider whether or not the components of your application will communicate using messages or using a more tightly coupled, connected approach such as DCOM or .NET remoting. Connected communication is easier to design and implement, but has limitations in terms of scalability, availability, and manageability.

Separating Inter- and Intra-Application Communication

Inter-application communication (in other words, communication with external services) should be implemented using a message-based model such as SOAP-based XML Web services or Microsoft Message Queuing. Internally, the components of your application may require a communication mechanism that provides high performance and specific capabilities such as transaction or security context flow. You can accomplish this using connected communication models such as DCOM. However, when transaction or identity flow is not required, you could use XML Web services between the tiers of your application. It is recommended that you use a message-based communication mechanism whenever possible in your application. This includes communication between the user interface layers, business processes, and the user interface, and between service interfaces and business layers.

Note: XML Web services do not currently support standards-based transactions or identity flow. Global XML Web Services Architecture (GXA) will address these issues by defining specifications for transactions and security. More information on GXA can be found at *http://msdn.microsoft.com/library/en-us/dnglobspec/html/wsspecsover.asp*.

The different requirements and constraints of inter-application communication and intra-application communication will drive most technology decisions. In many cases, it may not be a maintenance issue to have tightly coupled components that are built, deployed, and managed as a unit. However, in some cases it may be useful to view the different tiers of applications as services and strive to have the same loose coupling between application tiers that is found between unrelated services. Figure 3.5 illustrates this concept.

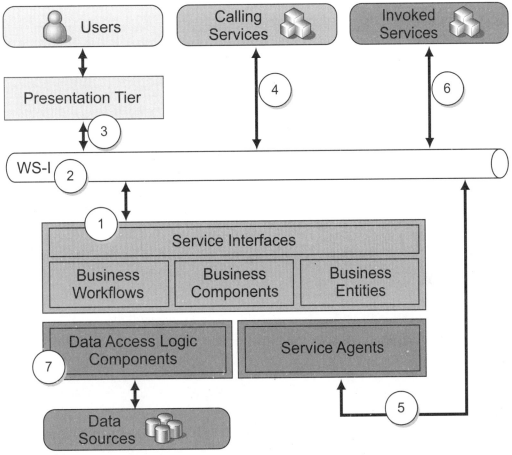

Figure 3.5
Implementing communication between the presentation and business tiers using the message bus

Figure 3.5 shows that the application is designed as a service (1) that is accessed using a message bus (2). The presentation tier (3) uses the same communication as other calling services (4), potentially invoking other services (6) directly as well. Service agents (5) invoke other services by using the message bus as well (6). Communication with the data components is most realistically implemented using other communication mechanisms (7), unless the data needs to be exposed for data-to-data or process-to-data scenarios, in which case the data sources would also be accessed by using the message bus.

Using the same communication bus between tiers and services leads to a more modular design of the system, where other services may choose finer-grained pieces of functionality to integrate with. It also leads to a higher level of independence between the teams and platforms used for each tier.

Viewing tiers as services may be a compelling long-term vision for a system, but it may pose several design challenges:

- The business layers may rely on having context such as security information provided by the user interface, which may be unavailable when trying to invoke the same logic from an application.

- The message bus or communication has to support all the requirements of intra-application communication, such as transaction flow, efficient transfer of large payloads, high throughput and low latency, and transfer of rich exception information. Standards are evolving in all these areas, but the development model still required to use them is not transparent.

- It is tough to design the same level of resiliency and availability between UI and the business layers as the level expected between services. The communication between the user interface and the business tiers is probably the best place to design communication based on the same standards used between services. The communication between data and business tiers of an application is still territory for efficient but non-generic communication mechanisms.

If your goal is to have a more traditional application design, and if service integration is only a small aspect of the overall architecture, you may want to use the Web services, standards-based message exchanges for integration purposes only and use DCOM or .NET remoting for intra application communication, as shown in Figure 3.6.

In Figure 3.6, the presentation, business, and data tiers communicate with each other using efficient but probably nonstandard communication mechanisms. The use of standards-based and message-based communication is left for integration purposes, where service interfaces accept calls from potential external callers (3 and 4) and service agents make the calls to other services (5 and 6).

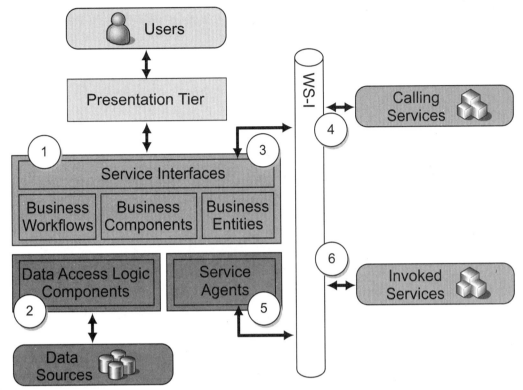

Figure 3.6
Using the message bus for integration purposes only

Message-based communication, especially when implemented asynchronously on a store-and-forward transport, provides the best choice of communication for integration, but the gain is not for free: You must consider many design issues before you can implement it correctly.

Advantages of Asynchronous Message-Based Communication

Using an asynchronous message-based communication mechanism provides the following advantages:

- **Scalability and availability.** Message-based communication provides better scalability and availability (both in terms of robustness and resiliency) for your application and service. With message-based communication, you can better utilize your hardware resources and isolate your application from software or infrastructure failures.

- **Location transparency.** Message-based communication also provides true transparency of remote functionality, because it doesn't assume that a connection is present and that a message can always be sent.

- **Similarity to business models.** Real-world business processes are mostly modeled asynchronously, in terms of exchanges between parties and users. Using message-based communications may provide a cleaner mapping between your requirements and the behavior of your application.

- **SLA isolation.** It is easier to define and keep SLAs in terms of message exchanges. Using message-based communication also enables you to isolate internal bottlenecks in your internal business processes or external services from the performance SLAs you want to guarantee to your users.

- **Transport agnostic.** An application or service correctly designed for message-based communication can easily take advantage of new messaging technologies as they appear.

Disadvantages of Message-Based Communication

Message-based communication comes at a premium. As you read this list of design considerations, keep in mind the preceding advantages—the effort in designing message-based communications pays itself off easily during the lifetime of the service or application. Disadvantages of message-based communication are:

- **Deterministic outcome.** In a connected scenario, you know whether a request succeeded or failed at the end of it. In message-based communication, you need to consider extra states in which no return message has been received. This means that you have to manage *conversation state* in addition to your normal business logic (for example, you may have to log sent messages for later processing in case a response is not received).

- **Message correlation.** Because there is no automatic pairing of messages sent and received, you will need to implement a correlation mechanism that identifies that a certain message involves a particular instance of a business process or conversation. You can implement this correlation in the messaging transport (for example, by setting correlation IDs in Message Queuing messages) or in the business data. Implementing the correlation in the business data will help you to easily change messaging transport and to achieve idempotency of business processes more easily.

- **Message delay.** Messages may arrive later than expected. You have to implement your business logic such that it can deal with messages that never arrive. You also should design your message receipt logic to make sure the message is still valid when received. For example, if you are receiving an order, you could specify a *drop dead* time after which the order will not be processed. Consider a case in which your catalog prices have changed between the order submission by the caller and the message receipt. In this case, you will either need to specify whether the order is processed with the new prices, the prices at the time, or not processed at all. It may be useful in some cases for the message to include critical *reference data* it is based upon—such as the prices of the products — so your business logic can actually compare and make more fine-grained decisions on what to do with a message.

- **Transaction flow.** Message-based communication implies a different transaction model. If you are using a transactional transport (such as transactional Message Queuing queues), a transaction commit will make sure that the *send* operation is performed. You will not be able to send a transactional message *and* receive its response in the context of one atomic transaction. This means that you will need to manage conversations involving multiple exchanges in a long-running transaction, and expose the appropriate compensation activities.

- **Repeated messages.** Your logic will need to handle a special case in which messages may arrive more than once. You can implement this by designing your processes and logic to be idempotent when receiving the same message more than once. For example, in a payment processing service that debits funds from a customer's account and credits them to the retailer's account, you must avoid transferring the money for a particular purchase multiple times if the payment request message is received more than once. You can avoid this problem by requiring a transaction ID to be supplied with the payment request and ignoring all subsequent requests with the same transaction ID. You can also achieve idempotency by specifying the old and new data for operations that will update the database. In this case, receiving a message to change the shipped attribute of an order from No to Yes twice is not a problem (if your business logic determines so).

- **Message sequence.** If you are expecting more than one incoming message, you may not receive the messages in the expected sequence. In this case, you can either handle this in the conversation state or in your business logic. You can force sequencing in your business logic by making the conversation depend on acknowledgements. For example, you could determine that all order update messages have an ID which you have provided to the issuer. This design technique defeats some of the advantages of message-based communication, so use it only when required.

Scenarios for Message-Based Communication

You should design an interface to your application or service to be message-based (such as when using SOAP) and based on asynchronous store-and-forward mechanisms such as Message Queuing when:

- You are implementing a business system that represents a medium- to long-term investment; for example, when building a service that will be exposed to and used by partners for a long period of time.

- You are implementing large scale systems with high availability characteristics.

- You are building a service that you want to isolate from other services it uses and from services it is exposed to.

- You expect the communication of both endpoints to be sporadically unavailable, as in the case of wireless networks or applications that can be used offline.

Synchronicity

It is common to think of message-based communication as an asynchronous model. For example, it is evident that two applications communicating with each other using Message Queuing are doing so using messages. However, message-based communication can also be encapsulated in a synchronous programming model (for example, by using Web service proxies generated by Microsoft Visual Studio® .NET), in which the client waits for a response message. In this case, the application developer can gain the benefits of message-based communication without having to deal with the complexities of programming in an asynchronous model.

For more information, see "Architectural Options for Asynchronous Workflow" on MSDN (*http://msdn.microsoft.com/library/default.asp?url=/library/en-us/dnbda/html /bdadotnetarch12.asp?frame=true*).

Choosing Technologies for Asynchronous Communications

A number of approaches can be used for asynchronous communication, including message-based approaches such as Message Queuing and XML Web services, and connected technologies such as .NET remoting and DCOM. Of these approaches, queuing technologies offer the greatest level of flexibility and richness of features. Message Queuing provides a store-and-forward messaging transport for use in applications. In addition to scalability and availability, Message Queuing provides many development options to assist the application's development and deployment in many scenarios.

Message Queuing provides the following options and features:

- Internet store-and-forward messaging.

- Transactional messaging with exactly once message delivery guarantee.

- Cluster-based storage for high availability.

You can find more information on the next version of Message Queuing at *http:// www.microsoft.com/msmq/MSMQ3.0_whitepaper_draft.doc*

When using Message Queuing, you will need to determine the endpoint technology and the message format. The following endpoints and formats are available:

- Sending and receiving endpoints

You can develop code that uses the objects in the System.Messaging namespace, or you can use the Message Queuing trigger service to listen for messages. If you control both endpoints and have no requirements around message format, you can use Enterprise Services Queued Components, which completely encapsulate Message Queuing–related development. Your endpoints can also include COM-based applications, BizTalk Server ports, and bridges to MQSeries and other messaging technologies.

- Formats

  You can use SOAP, binary, and Microsoft ActiveX® formats. SOAP is used for maximum interoperability, binary is used for message size efficiency, and ActiveX is used for interoperability with COM-based senders and listeners. Because it is COM-based, MSMQ Triggers requires the use of ActiveX formatting. Queued Components send messages in an opaque DCE RPC format, which is kept transparent to the developer.

Enterprise Services Queued Components

You can use Enterprise Services Queued Components when:

- You control both the sender and receiver of the message.
- Your receiving component is a Serviced Component.
- You don't care about the format of the message (it will be an opaque RPC NDR binary format).

Queued Components have these advantages:

- You can use Enterprise Services role-based authorization with no need to do extra development to sign the message on the sender.
- You can use the built-in retry mechanism in Message Queuing to make sure that messages are eventually run.
- You can use exception classes to get notification of errors so you can take alternate actions.
- Messages can be sent by both COM and .NET senders.
- You can easily work with transactions transparently with the Enterprise Services model.

Message Queuing Triggers

Message Queuing triggers provide a listener service. Use Message Queuing triggers when:

- You don't control the senders.
- You need to trigger an .exe file or COM component when a message arrives.
- Your message format can be ActiveX.
- You are prepared to implement the receiver function as a .NET-based component that will be invoked using COM Interop.

Custom Receivers

Writing a custom receiver gives you the greatest degree of control over format, retry behavior, exception management, and so on. However, it is not recommended that you develop your own listener service because doing so requires skills in asynchronous communication management, multithreading, security, and exception management. If you build your own receiver service, you should test it extensively before deployment.

Alternative Asynchronous Technologies

As an alternative to using Message Queuing, you can also create an XML Web service proxy with Visual Studio .NET, in which case each method exposed by the Web service can be called asynchronously using the *Begin*<method name> method and specifying a callback function.

You can also use callbacks to implement asynchronous method invocations over .NET remoting channels. For more information about implementing asynchronous operations with .NET remoting, see the Asynchronous Remoting section in the .NET Framework documentation on MSDN (*http://msdn.microsoft.com/library /default.asp?url=/library/en-us/cpguide/html/cpconasynchronousremoting.asp*).

Choosing Technologies for Synchronous Communications

.NET provides many options for synchronous communication. Each option is defined as a combination of an endpoint (for example, IIS), a protocol (for example, HTTP), and a format (for example, SOAP). Each possible combination represents a *channel* through which communication can take place. You can also implement custom channels by defining your own combination of endpoint, protocol, and format.

Channels have many attributes, the importance of which depends on the components intercommunicating. These attributes include:

- Transaction context flow capability.
- Breadth of reach to different clients on different platforms.
- Security capabilities (authentication, authorization, and channel encryption).
- Protocol requirements over networking infrastructure.
- Efficiency as function of data type and size being transmitted.

Answering the following questions will help you choose a synchronous communication technology based on your requirements:

1. Do you need transaction flow or to flow Windows security context?

If so, use DCOM. Your endpoints will be hosted in Enterprise Services to take advantage of the transactions. The callee will be able to learn the identity of the original caller of the component by using the SecurityCallContext class.

Otherwise, move on to question 2.

2. Do you need broad reach?

If you need to expose your service in a standard way to ensure maximum reach, you can use SOAP and HTTP to implement XML Web services. You can expose Web services in two ways in Windows 2000: Using ASP.NET .asmx files or using the HTTP/SOAP remoting channel. Move on to question 4.

Otherwise, move on to question 3.

3. Do you need to authenticate the caller?

If you don't need transactions, security flow, or broad reach you can use .NET remoting channels. .NET remoting relies on IIS to perform authentication of the caller when calling over HTTP, so you will need to have an IIS endpoint if you need authentication.

If you don't need authentication, you can use any .NET remoting channel hosted in any process.

4. Do you need to implement façade code to expose your business functionality?

If you need to wrap your business logic in an extra façade, to perform extra validation, transformation, or maybe even caching, you can use ASP.NET Web services to easily implement functions that are callable by SOAP.

If you don't need an extensive façade layer, then you can expose your types directly as Web services. Note that you cannot expose Enterprise Services classes directly. If your business components are Serviced Components, you will need to create a façade layer with ASP.NET Web services or remoting classes on Windows 2000.

Note: Using DCOM with the latest fixes will enable you to establish communication through only one known port. For more information, see the following Knowledge Base articles:

Q154596—HOWTO: Configure RPC Dynamic Port Allocation to Work with Firewall (*http://support.microsoft.com/support/kb/articles/q154/5/96.asp*)

Q312960—Cannot Set Fixed Endpoint for a COM+ Application (*http://support.microsoft.com/default.aspx?scid=kb;en-us;q312960*)

For more information about deciding between XML Web services and .NET remoting, see "Choosing Communication Options in .NET" in the .NET Framework documentation on MSDN (*http://msdn.microsoft.com/library/default.asp?url=/library/en-us/cpguide/html/cpconchoosingcommunicationoptionsinnet.asp*).

The following sources provide more information on .NET remoting:

- "Exposing Existing Code as a Web Service Using the .NET Framework" (*http://msdn.microsoft.com/library/default.asp?url=/library/en-us/dnbda/html/bdadotnetwebservice1.asp?frame=true*)

- "An Introduction to Microsoft .NET Remoting Framework" (*http://msdn.microsoft.com/library/default.asp?url=/library/en-us/dndotnet/html/introremoting.asp?frame=true*)

- The DotNetRemoting.cc Web site (*http://www.dotnetremoting.cc*)
- "Performance Comparison: Exposing Existing Code as a Web Service" (*http://msdn.microsoft.com/library/default.asp?url=/library/en-us/dnbda/html/bdadotnetarch11.asp?frame=true*)
- *Advanced .NET Remoting* by Ingo Rammer (ISBN 1590590252)

Recommendations for Communications

When implementing your service and application, consider these recommendations:

- Cut call chains with queues and caches as much as possible. Doing so will enhance the scalability and availability of the overall solution.
- Push out asynchronous boundaries close to the user, service interfaces, and service agents, to isolate your service from external dependencies.
- If you need to expose functionality as a synchronous operation, evaluate whether you can wrap an internally asynchronous operation as described in the following discussion.

Encapsulating Asynchronous Communication in Synchronous Requests

Your application design should strive to use asynchronous communications as much as possible. However, in some cases, it is reasonable or unavoidable for the client to expect a synchronous response. You may also want to rely on fully asynchronous design only if the service you are calling doesn't meet your expectations in terms of response times. This pattern applies mostly to implementing service agents.

You can design your components such that you use asynchronous operations, yet you provide a synchronous interface to callers. The basic design for achieving this is as follows:

1. The caller submits a synchronous request to a component.
2. The component receives the request and, at minimum, creates or identifies an ID or cookie to unequivocally identify this request, optimally backed up by a database entry.
3. The server submits an asynchronous request to the service.
4. The component sets itself to wait for a response message, with a timeout.
5. If the component receives the message in time, it builds the response and returns it to the synchronous caller.
6. If the component doesn't receive the message in time, it returns a "boilerplate" response with the request ID to the caller, or an exception that the caller can handle. The server component should then deactivate.

7. You then have two options for getting the result to the caller:

- The caller optionally then invokes a server component (maybe a different function in the same component) to poll for the result after some time (seconds or minutes) based on the request ID. If the caller is a human user, it is common practice to entertain him or her with some graphic animation.

- The server notifies the caller using an asynchronous mechanism, such as a user notification (e-mail, Windows Messenger, or a pager message) or sends a message back to the client so it can display the right result. In this case, either the application or the user has to have an addressable "message sink," such as an e-mail or a Message Queuing message path. If you are using Message Queuing, you should correlate the return message using the correlation ID. The Instant Notification reference architecture is available on MSDN at *http://msdn.microsoft.com/library/en-us/dnenra/html/enraelp.asp*.

Communication Format, Schema, and Protocol

The format in which you send and receive data and the schema of the data you exchange are important factors when designing your application communication.

The following factors influence the format and schema:

- Do you control both endpoints of the communication? If so, you can choose formats and protocols that optimize performance and provide extra features (such as security or transaction flow) at the cost of broad interoperability. This is the case when you are communicating the tiers of your application and you consider all tiers to be strongly related or coupled.

- Do you want your service to be accessible to external callers inside or outside the organization? If so, you should strive to choose widely accepted standards for protocols (such as TCP), formats (for example SOAP), and even schemas (for example, using schemas available in www.uddi.org), especially for service interfaces and service agents. If the service you are contacting or your own communication does not rely on standards, you may need to use bridges or extra translation layers between the endpoints.

A Look Ahead

Service communication based on industry standards is quickly maturing, and Microsoft is providing facilities in its next generation of products to maker it even easier to expose and consume business functionality through standard mechanisms.

The following links will provide you some insight into what the future looks like:

- "COM+ Web Services: The Check-Box Route to XML Web Services" (*http://msdn.microsoft.com/library/default.asp?url=/library/en-us/dndotnet/html/comwscheckb.asp?frame=true*)

- "The Windows .NET Server Application Environment (*http://msdn.microsoft.com/library/default.asp?url=/library/en-us/dnnetserv/html/windowsnetserver.asp*)

- "An Introduction to GXA: Global XML Web Services Architecture" (*http://msdn.microsoft.com/library/default.asp?url=/library/en-us/dngxa/html/gloxmlws500.asp?frame=true*)

- "Reliable XML Web Services" (*http://msdn.microsoft.com/library/default.asp?url=/library/en-us/dnexxml/html/xml11192001.asp?frame=true*)

- *http://msdn.microsoft.com/webservices*

- *http://www.gotdotnet.com/team/XMLwebservices/default.aspx*

- *http://www.gotdotnet.com/team/XML_wsspecs/*

- *http://discuss.develop.com/*

What's Next?

This chapter discussed organizational policies for security, operational management, and communications. Chapter 4, "*Physical Deployment and Operational Requirements,*" describes strategies for deploying your application in a physical environment, and discusses ways to achieve operational requirements.

Physical Deployment and Operational Requirements

This chapter describes the different options available when deploying your application in a physical environment and suggests strategies for meeting the operational (nonfunctional) requirements of your application.

Chapter Contents

This chapter includes the following sections:

- Deploying Application Components
- Common Deployment Patterns
- Operational Requirements
- Feedback and Support

Deploying Application Components

So far, this guide has described the application architecture in terms of *logical* layers. It is important to remember that these layers are simply a convenient way to describe the different kinds of functionality in the application. They are conceptual divisions rather than a physical deployment pattern. How you deploy your *physical* application layers into *tiers* is driven by how the layers interact with each other and the different requirements they have in terms of security, operations, and communication.

Your application will eventually be deployed into a physical infrastructure. In some cases, the application architect will be able to define the physical infrastructure, but in many other cases, the IT department will determine it. Physical deployment patterns are usually decided through negotiation between the IT department and application developers driven by the solution architect.

In any deployment scenario, you must:

- Know your target physical deployment environment early, from the planning stage of the lifecycle.
- Clearly communicate what environmental constraints drive software design and architecture decisions.
- Clearly communicate what software design decisions require certain infrastructure attributes.

Physical Deployment Environments

Physical deployment environments vary depending on the kind of application being deployed, the user base of the application, scalability, performance requirements, organizational policies, and other factors. A number of infrastructure patterns with similar characteristics can be identified for specific kinds of applications, particularly Internet-based solutions. For example, the Microsoft® Systems Architecture Internet Data Center documentation describes a recommended physical deployment pattern for Web-based applications, as shown in Figure 4.1. For more information, see "Microsoft Systems Architecture: Internet Data Center" on Microsoft TechNet (*http://www.microsoft.com/technet/treeview/default.asp?url=/technet /itsolutions/idc/default.asp*).

Just as an application is made up of components and services, the infrastructure that hosts an application can be thought of as consisting of a number of infrastructure building blocks, referred to as physical tiers. These physical tiers represent the physical divisions between the components of your application, and may or may not map directly to the *logical* tiers or layers used to abstract the different kinds of functionality in the application. The physical tiers may be separated by firewalls or other security boundaries to create different units of trust or security contexts. There are two main families of physical tiers, farms and clusters. Farms consist of identically configured and extendable sets of servers sharing the workload. Clusters are specialized sets of computers controlling a shared resource such as a data store, designed to handle failures of individual nodes gracefully.

A number of common infrastructure building blocks can be found in many application deployment environments.

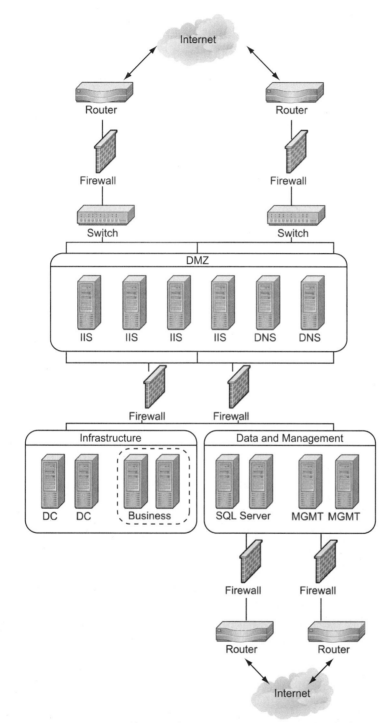

Figure 4.1
The Internet Data Center architecture

Web Farms

A Web farm is a load-balanced array of Web servers. A number of technologies can be used to implement the load-balancing mechanism, including hardware solutions such as those offered by Cisco and Nortel switches and routers, and software solutions such as Network Load Balancing. In either case, the principle is the same: A user makes a request for an Internet resource using a URL, and the incoming request is serviced by one of the servers in the farm. Because the requests are load balanced between the servers in the farm, a server failure will not cause the Web site to cease functioning. The requests can be load balanced with no affinity (that is, each request can be serviced by any of the servers in the farm), or with affinity based on the requesting computer's IP address, in which case requests from a particular range of IP addresses are always balanced to the same Web server. In general, you should try to implement load balancing with no affinity to provide the highest level of scalability and availability.

For more information about how Web farms are implemented in Microsoft Systems Architecture Internet Data Center, see the *Internet Data Center Reference Architecture Guide* on TechNet (*http://www.microsoft.com/technet/treeview/default.asp?url=/technet /itsolutions/idc/rag/ragc02.asp*).

When designing a Web-based user interface that will be deployed in a Web farm, you should consider the following issues:

- **Session state**. In Active Server Pages (ASP)–based applications, you should avoid depending on the ASP Session object for state data between requests because each new request may be sent to a different server. ASP holds session data in-process, so the same session data will not exists on all servers in the farm. With Microsoft ASP.NET-based solutions, this limitation is removed. ASP.NET-based applications can be configured to store their session state out of process on a remote Microsoft Internet Information Services (IIS) server, or in a Microsoft SQL Server™ database. ASP.NET also provides an easy way to configure "cookieless" sessions, so that the Session object can be used even when the user's browser does not support cookies. For more information about using the Session object in ASP.NET–based applications, see "ASP.NET Session State" on MSDN (*http://msdn.microsoft.com/library/default.asp?url=/library/en-us/dnaspnet/html /asp12282000.asp*).

- **ViewState**. ViewState is used in ASP.NET pages to maintain user interface consistency between post-back requests. For example, a page may contain a drop-down list that automatically posts the page's data back to the Web server for server-side processing. ViewState is used to ensure that the other controls on the page are not reset to their original default values after the post-back. ViewState is implemented as a hidden form field and can be secured using encryption. In a Web farm environment, this requires consistency between settings in the machine.config file on each server in the farm. For more information about using ViewState in a Web farm, see "Taking a Bite Out of ASP.NET ViewState" on MSDN (*http:// msdn.microsoft.com/library/default.asp?url=/library /en-us/dnaspnet/html/asp11222001.asp*).

- **SSL Communications**. If you are using Secure Sockets Layer (SSL) to encrypt traffic between the client and the Web farm, you need to ensure that affinity is maintained between the client and the particular Web server with which it establishes the SSL session key. To maximize scalability and performance, you may choose to use a separate farm for HTTPS connections, allowing you to load balance HTTP requests with no affinity, but maintain "sticky sessions" for HTTPS requests.

Application Farms

Applications farms are conceptually similar to Web farms, but they are used to load balance requests for business components across multiple application servers. Application farms are used to host business components, in particular those components that use .NET Enterprise Services (COM+) services such as transaction management, loosely coupled events, and other component services. If the components are designed to be stateless, you can implement the load-balancing mechanism of the application farm using Network Load Balancing, because each request can be serviced by any of the identically configured servers in the farm. Alternatively, you can implement an application farm using Component Load Balancing (CLB), a function provided by Microsoft Application Center 2000. For more information about CLB, see the Application Center home page (*http://www.microsoft.com /applicationcenter/*).

Database Clusters

Database clusters are used to provide high availability of a database server. Windows Clustering provides the basis for a clustered SQL Server–based solution and supports two or four node clusters. Clusters can be configured in Active/Passive mode (where one member of the cluster acts as a failover node), or Active/Active mode (where each cluster member controls its own databases while acting as a failover node for the other cluster member).

For more information about implementing clustered SQL Server–based solutions, see Chapter 5 of the *Internet Data Center Reference Architecture Guide* (*http:// www.microsoft.com/technet/treeview/default.asp?url=/technet/itsolutions/idc/rag /ragc05.asp*).

When designing a .NET–based application that will connect to a database hosted in a cluster, you should take extra care to open and close connections as you need them, and not hold on to open connection objects. This will ensure that ADO.NET can reconnect to the active database server node in case of a failover in the cluster.

EAI Clusters

Microsoft BizTalk® Server relies on four SQL Server databases to store its messaging and orchestration data. These databases can benefit from Windows Clustering for high availability. For general information about clustering BizTalk Server, see "High-Availability Solutions Using Microsoft Windows 2000 Cluster Service" in the BizTalk Server 2002 documentation on MSDN (*http://msdn.microsoft.com/library /default.asp?url=/library/en-us/dnbiz2k2/html/bts_2002clustering.asp*). For information about clustering BizTalk Server in the Internet Data Center infrastructure, see the Internet Data Center Reference Architecture Guide.

BizTalk Server Orchestration persists its schedule data in a SQL Server database. Because the enterprise application integration (EAI) tier is a unit of trust, this data store should be considered private, and it should not be directly accessible to any software component outside the tier. You will need to decide whether you want to deploy the integration functionality in a perimeter network (also known as demilitarized zone, or DMZ) that can interact with the Internet, or on the internal network, which provides better connectivity with the organization's services and applications. *The Internet Data Center Reference Architecture Guide* discusses these issues in detail.

By introducing multiple BizTalk "Receive" and "Worker" servers around a single shared work queue (itself hosted in a clustered SQL Server environment), you can increase the performance and throughput of the BizTalk cluster as needed and achieve high availability.

Your physical environment will probably include some, if not all, of these common infrastructure building blocks, on which your application components will be deployed.

Rich Clients

Another possibility is to deploy components to rich clients. It is assumed that rich clients are running the Microsoft Windows® operating system and that they are able to run .NET components. You can also create a rich user interface through integration with applications such as those in the Microsoft Office suite.

In most enterprises, using rich clients implies:

- The ability to authenticate users through Microsoft Active Directory® directory service (thus having access to a Windows Identity and Principal).
- Access to richer state management options, including maintaining session-related state in memory. (In high scalability and availability scenarios, it is not a good idea to keep in-memory state on the server.)
- The ability to work offline.

Rich clients are also better targets for the user interface of complex operations.

It is important to thoroughly test rich client applications, because the security context that they run under is typically constrained by the user policy and any code access security policy present on the computer.

Thin Clients

Thin clients usually manage HTML or even simpler UI models, so they are not typically considered a deployment target for your components. You can include .NET controls in HTML pages, but in that case you are simply using the browser as a deployment vehicle, and should consider your user interface to be rich.

Planning the Physical Location of Application Components

One of the most important decisions you need to make as an application architect is where you will physically deploy the components in your application. As with all aspects of application architecture, physical deployment decisions involve trade-offs between performance, reusability, security, and other factors. Organizational policies regarding security, communications, and operational management also affect the deployment decisions you make.

It is common to wonder whether different pieces of interacting software should be deployed together, especially if they are part of the same service or application. There is no one correct answer to the question of whether to distribute your components across separate physical tiers. However, there are certain factors to consider that can help you reach a decision about deploying components together or deploying them separately.

When deciding on the physical architecture of your application, you should keep one thing in mind: distributing your components results in a performance hit. There are a number of good reasons to distribute components, but doing so always affects performance negatively. Distributing components can improve the scalability and manageability of your application, lower financial costs, and so on.

In general, choosing a deployment consists of three main stages involving both infrastructure and application architects:

1. **Identifying the minimum topologies that work.** Early in the design phase, you must determine what conditions your application requires if it is to work at all. For example, your service agents may need to call out to Web services on the Internet. The application will not work if you cannot establish the appropriate outgoing communication. You should make a list of these typed of "must have" requirements.

2. **Applying restrictions and enforcing requirements.** A requirement from your application design (for example, the use of Microsoft Distributed Transaction Coordinator [DTC] transactions) translates to a set of requirements for the infrastructure (for example, the DTC uses remote procedure call [RPC] ports to communicate, so those must be open in the internal firewalls).

   The infrastructure architect should make a list of "must have" requirements for his or her data center similar to the one you made in the previous stage. Then you should start at the infrastructure and follow the same process of applying restrictions and identifying requirements. A design characteristic of the infrastructure may be considered unchangeable, and it may affect how you design your application. For example, the infrastructure may not provide access to corporate domain users on an external Web farm due to security. This is a design constraint that precludes you from authenticating users of your application with Windows authentication.

As in the previous step, these requirements and constraints should be laid out early in the design cycle before building the application. Sometimes the requirements of the application and those of the infrastructure will conflict. The solution architect should arbitrate the decision.

3. **Optimizing the infrastructure and application.** After you have determined the requirements and constraints for the infrastructure and application and have resolved all conflicts, you may find that many characteristics of both the application and infrastructure design have been left unspecified. Both the application and infrastructure should then be tuned to improve their characteristics in these areas. For example, if the infrastructure architect has provided access through firewall ports for Message Queuing, but your application is not using it, he or she may improve security by closing those ports. On the other hand, the infrastructure may be agnostic to the authentication mechanism you use with your database, so you may choose to use integrated Windows or SQL Server authentication depending on your application security model.

Factors Affecting Component Deployment

A number of quantitative and qualitative factors influence the decision to deploy components together or distribute them. These factors can be grouped around abilities of your application and are closely related to the policies: security, operational management, and communication:

Security

In deciding how to deploy components, you should consider the following security factors:

- **Location of sensitive resources and data**. Your security policy may determine that certain libraries, encryption keys, or other resources cannot be deployed in particular security contexts (for example, on a Web server or on users' desktop computers).

  You may also want to prevent access to sensitive resources from components deployed in less trusted physical zones. For example, you may not want to allow access to your database from a Web farm, but may instead require a separate layer of components behind a firewall to perform database access.

- **Increased security boundaries.** By physically distributing components over several tiers, you increase the number of obstacles that a potential attacker must overcome to compromise the system.

- **Security context of running code.** Physically distributing your components may cause them to run in drastically different security contexts. For example, a remote component tier usually runs under a service account, whereas Web tier components may run under the authenticated user account. If you distribute your components, you will have to decide how you will manage identity flow, impersonation, and auditing of actions performed under service accounts.

Management

The management factors affecting component deployment are as follows:

- **Management and monitoring**. To make it easier to manage and monitor a piece of your application logic that is used by multiple consumers, you may want to deploy it in only one place where everyone can access it. For example, you may decide to deploy a business component that is used by multiple user interfaces in a single central location.

  Backup and restore capabilities may not be available for all physical tiers of your application, so you should make sure that critical databases and queues are accessible to your backup and restore solution.

- **Component location dependencies**. Some of your components may rely on existing software or hardware and must be physically located on the same computer. For example, your application may use a connection to a proprietary network that can only be established from a particular computer in the existing physical environment. In this case, some of your application logic needs to be deployed on that particular server.

- **Licensing**. Some libraries and adaptors cannot be deployed freely without incurring extra costs. Also, some products are licensed on a per-CPU basis. CPU-based licensing makes it more efficient to dedicate fewer CPUs to such a product rather than to share many CPUs among many products and tasks.

- **Political factors**. In some organizations, political factors may influence where you locate certain functionality. For example, a group within an organization may want ownership of a particular piece of a service or application.

Performance, Availability, and Scalability

Your decision to deploy components together or to distribute them should take into account the following factors involving performance, availability, and scalability:

- **Complexity of interfaces**. It is more efficient to distribute components whenever the interface between them is designed to require fewer information exchanges or calls with more data. Such an interface is usually referred to as "chunky" (as opposed to a "chatty" interface). The granularity of interaction between your components thus dramatically affects performance and how state is managed, with the related impact on scalability and availability.

- **Communications**. You will need to move your atomic transaction root to a place where it can communicate with all resource managers. DTC uses RPC to communicate through port 135 and a dynamic range of other ports. You may not want to open these ports on a firewall that separates your Web farm from your business components.

- **Availability**. You can improve your application's availability by physically separating business-critical activities from other computers and components that could fail. For example, you may choose to implement long-running business processes on a separate tier of clustered servers, so that a failure in your Web farm does not prevent business processes from being completed.

- **Performance**. As mentioned before, distributing components results in the performance hit of serializing and deserializing data and establishing network connections. However, you may improve the overall scalability of your application by separating units of work that affect each other.

- **Hardware capabilities**. Specific types of servers are better suited to perform particular tasks and host particular products and technologies. For example, Web servers are typically computers with good memory and processing power. However, they do not tend to have robust storage capabilities (such as RAID mirroring, and so on) that can be replaced rapidly in the event of a hardware failure. Because of this, you shouldn't install a database with mission critical data on a computer that is intended as a Web server.

Distribution Boundaries Between Components

If you design your application according to the guidelines in chapters 2 and 3 of this guide, you will find that it is more efficient to deploy certain types of components together, whereas other types of components interact with their callers in a way better suited for remote access.

Planning User Interface Deployment

Deciding on a deployment location for the user interface components is very straightforward: You deploy Windows-based applications on the clients, and ASP.NET pages on Web servers.

User process components should be deployed together with the user interface components that they orchestrate. In Web environments, this means deploying the user process components on the IIS Web servers, and for Windows clients this means deploying the user process components with the Windows Forms–based application. The user process components should be deployed in a .NET assembly that is separate from the user interface logic to facilitate reuse and easy maintenance.

Planning Business Component Deployment

The question of where to deploy business logic usually provokes strong feelings and debate among application and infrastructure architects. Although there are many possible physical deployment patterns for business components, you should consider the following recommendations:

- Business components that are used synchronously by user interfaces or user process components can be deployed with the user interface to maximize performance and ease operational management. This approach is more appropriate in Web-based applications than in Windows-based applications because you would probably not want to deploy your business components to every desktop. However, even in Web scenarios, if you want to isolate your business logic so it is not in the same trust boundary as the user interface, or if you need to reuse the business logic for multiple user interfaces, you may choose to deploy the business components on a separate tier of application servers and use a communications technology such as .NET remoting, DCOM, or SOAP over HTTP to make them accessible to the user interface logic. In Web scenarios, the inclusion of a firewall between the user interface and the application servers may add configuration and management complexity.

- Business processes that are implemented as a service, and are therefore communicated with asynchronously, should generally be deployed on a separate physical tier. Usually, asynchronous services should have their own application cluster, separate from other synchronous application servers, so that they form their own trust zone. This is true when implementing a business workflow using custom .NET components or BizTalk Server orchestration. The business components used "internally" by the service should generally be deployed on the same physical tier as the service interface components used to call into the service.

- Service agent components should generally be deployed with the business components or processes that use them. However, you may want to deploy service agents on a separate physical tier if the tier handles communication with an external service over the Internet and you want to isolate the Internet-facing communication in a different security context from your business components.

- Business entity components and strongly typed DataSets should generally be deployed with the code that uses them. Calling business entities remotely is usually not a good design choice from a performance perspective, because they tend to be stateful and expose "chatty" interfaces, which would cause a great deal of network traffic in a remote deployment scenario.

Business components manage no persistent state, so you are not constrained to deploying them in a particular physical farm or cluster. Potentially, you could deploy them in multiple places, including a Web farm facing the intranet, an EAI cluster, and another farm facing the intranet.

Planning Service Interface and Service Agent Deployment

Service interfaces and service agent components receive calls from, and make calls to, external applications and services. These external applications and services may be located within the organization's network, in a zone that shares security and management policies, or they may be located outside the organization, probably requiring communication over the intranet or extranet.

Service interfaces can be deployed together with the business components and workflows they expose, or they can be deployed remotely. The criteria for deciding whether to deploy service interfaces together with the business logic are similar to those used when deciding where to deploy the user interface. If the service interface requires a connection to the Internet or a less trusted environment, the extra network hop may provide the extra security required. Having your service interfaces deployed remotely from your business components may allow two Web farms (one for ASP.NET-based UIs, and one for XML Web services) to call into the same application farm that hosts your business components.

Service agents pose a similar set of decisions, except that these components call services instead of receiving calls. Common infrastructure designs may limit the servers from which outgoing HTTP calls are made.

Planning Business Workflow Deployment

It is recommended that you deploy any BizTalk EAI clusters in a set of computers separate from the servers hosting any ASP.NET user interfaces and business components used by the UI. Doing so enables you to optimize processor usage for the typically asynchronous business workflow tasks and provide management processes that are adequate for BizTalk, Message Queuing, and the other specific technologies business workflows rely on.

It is important to decide whether to deploy the business components and data access components used by the business workflow into the same cluster. It is common to do so because the business workflows are usually deployed in a secure environment. However, deploying the same business components in multiple places adds complexity to the management processes, so it is generally recommended that you separate the following into distinct assemblies:

- Business components called by UI components
- Business components used only from business workflows or other business components

You should then deploy the appropriate assembly (or set of assemblies) with the business workflows or Web/component farms. This mechanism provides greater flexibility, better performance, and easier management for larger applications. However, it is suitable only if you can easily identify distinct business activities and components for use from the UI and from the business workflows.

Planning Data Access Component Deployment

Application data is nearly always stored on a dedicated database server, which for all but the most simple of applications should be clustered to ensure high availability. In Web applications, this database server should be in a VLAN somewhere behind the second firewall of the perimeter network to protect your data.

Deploying data access components with the components that use them yields the following advantages:

- Data transfers will be optimized because cross-process marshalling is avoided.
- Transactions involving business processes and data access components do not need to travel through firewalls, which means that extra ports do not need to be opened.
- Distributing components adds transaction failure nodes.
- Deploying components together guarantees automatic security context flow, so there is no need to set principal objects or reauthenticate remoting channels. Doing so also enables you to leverage code-access security to restrict which assemblies can call your data access components.

Data access components are usually used by business components, but may also be used from user interface components and user process components. For Web scenarios, it is recommended that you deploy them together with the user interface if your user interface takes advantage of DataReader streaming. However, you may not want to do so for various reasons, including:

- You want to prevent direct network access to your data sources from your Web farms for security reasons (this is a common reason to deploy the components separately). In such cases, you should deploy data access components in a physical business tier (and therefore a separate security context) and invoke them remotely from your Web tier.
- You want to use the data access components from both business components and the user interface components, but do not want to deploy duplicate components in two locations.

Each data source will have its own communication requirements for accessing it. For more information about accessing SQL Server over a firewall, see the ".NET Data Access Architecture Guide" on MSDN (*http://msdn.microsoft.com/library/en-us /dnbda/html/daag.asp*).

Partitioning Your Application or Service into Assemblies

.NET assemblies are units of deployment—a .NET assembly is deployed and versioned as a unit. .NET provides rich versioning and deployment capabilities that allow for versioning policy enforcement after an application has been deployed, but you need to carefully plan assembly partitioning to take full advantage of them. The assemblies that you create and the way that you distribute the components among them have a long-term impact on how your application is developed, deployed, managed, updated, and maintained.

Many factors affect how you distribute your components into separate assemblies. The following recommendations will help you make the appropriate choices for your application size, team composition and distribution, and management processes:

- **Create a separate assembly for each component type**. Using separate assemblies for data access components, business components, service interfaces, business entities, and so on gives you basic flexibility for deployment and maintenance of the application.

- **Avoid deploying one assembly into multiple locations**. Deploying the same components in multiple places increases the complexity of your deployment and management processes, so carefully consider whether you can consolidate all deployments into one physical tier, or whether you should use more than one assembly for a particular component type.

- **Consider having more than one assembly per component type**. Not all components of the same type follow the same development and maintenance cycles. For example, you may have multiple service agent components abstracting service calls for multiple business partners. In this case, it may be better to create one assembly per business partner to simplify versioning. Consider the following factors when deciding whether to use more than one assembly per component type:

  - What components, services, or data sources the assembly deals with—you may want to have a different assembly for service agent components that deal with different business partners, for components that deal with a specific primary interop assembly, or for business components that will be invoked from the user interface or business workflow exclusively. Separating components based on where they are called from or what they call improves your application management because you won't need to redeploy components; it also prevents you from having unused code deployed in different places.

  - Data access components may deal with multiple data sources. Separating data access components that work with different data sources into different assemblies may be beneficial if the implementation accessing a particular data source changes frequently. Otherwise, it is recommended that you use only one data access component assembly to provide abstraction from the fact that you are working with multiple sources.

- **Separate shared types into separate assemblies**. Many components in your application may rely on the same types to perform their work. It is recommended that you separate the following types into their distinct assemblies:

- **Exceptions**. Many application layers may need to deal with the same exception types. If you factor out in a separate assembly the exceptions that all your application layers rely on, you will not need to deploy assemblies containing business logic where the logic is not needed.

- **Shared interfaces and base classes**. Your application may define interfaces for other developers to use, or for easy addition of logic after the application is deployed. Separating interfaces and base classes used by others into assemblies that are separate from your business logic implementation will prevent complex versioning bindings in case your implementation changes, and will let you share the assemblies with the interface definition without sharing the assembly with your organization's code to external developers.

- **Utility components**. Your application typically relies on a set of utility components or building blocks that encapsulate specific technologies or provide services that may be used by many application layers, such as data access helpers, exception management, and security frameworks. Factoring these into their own assemblies simplifies development, maintenance, and versioning.

- **Consider the impact on the development process**. Having a large number of assemblies adds flexibility for deployment and maintenance, but it may increase the complexity of the development process because more build references, projects, and versioning issues will need to be taken care of. However, using separate assemblies that deal with a particular technology may help to distribute the workload to the right developers with the right skills, and using multiple Microsoft Visual Studio® .NET projects may facilitate work across development teams. For detailed guidelines on how to partition assemblies with regard to complex development teams or assembly dependencies, see Chapter 3 of "Team Development with Visual Studio .NET and Visual SourceSafe" on MSDN (*http:// msdn.microsoft.com/library/?url=/library/en-us/dnbda/html/tdlg_rm.asp?frame=true*).

- **Avoid deploying unused code**. If you partition assemblies that may be invoked from multiple components and deploy them in multiple places, you may end up deploying unused code. Some organizations may consider this a security or intellectual property risk, so consider whether you can re-factor your assemblies so that a component is deployed only where it is needed. .NET assemblies have a very small footprint, so disk space is not an important consideration.

- **Use a factoring approach to assembly partitioning**. You may want to start your project by defining a base set of well-planned assemblies, and then use common re-factoring disciplines to drive the creation of further assemblies by analyzing change frequencies, dependencies, and the other factors outlined earlier in this chapter.

- **Enforce assembly partitioning with enterprise templates**. Visual Studio .NET Enterprise templates let you define and enforce policies that developers use when creating the application, including assembly structure and dependency. If you will be developing a large application or developing many applications with a similar architecture, consider creating or tailoring an enterprise template to suit your needs.

Packaging and Distributing Application Components

To distribute your application, you will need to choose a way to package it and deploy it. Visual Studio .NET provides multiple options for packaging your applications, including but not limited to Microsoft Windows Installer files and CAB files.

You can also deploy some .NET–based applications with no packaging by copying the right files to the destination, sending them through e-mail, or providing FTP downloads.

There are also other tools and Microsoft services which you can use to distribute your application. These include:

- Microsoft Application Center
- Microsoft Systems Management Server
- Microsoft Active Directory

Detailed guidance about choosing the right packaging mechanism for your application and using the right distribution technology is available in "Deploying .NET Applications: Lifecycle Guide" on MSDN (*http://msdn.microsoft.com/library /default.asp?url=/library/en-us/dnbda/html/DALGRoadmap.asp*)

Common Deployment Patterns

The deployment pattern a particular application uses is typically determined by the architect in a process that involves parties responsible for operations and development. Different organizations or software vendors will approach the problem differently, so there is no single approach to determining the infrastructure. This section discusses several deployment patterns for your components and considers their pros, cons, and requirements.

Many variations of deployment patterns are possible (for example, you may need to deploy Microsoft Mobile Information Server in your solution), but not all are described in this section. To understand specific deployment characteristics and requirements, see the Internet Data Center guidelines earlier in this chapter and the appropriate product documentation.

You should also note that you can combine deployment patterns. It is advisable to deploy each component of the solution in only one physical tier or farm, but for security reasons you may want to consider deploying the same component in multiple locations at the expense of manageability.

Note: In the discussion that follows, the figures reference component types, but not specific assemblies. To determine assembly partitioning, follow the guidelines provided earlier in this chapter.

These figures look slightly different from Figure 4.1, which illustrates the Internet Data Center architecture, in that they show individual firewall instances between farms. The physical firewall devices in Internet Data Center may host multiple firewall instances, which in turn makes the physical network layout look different. All deployment patterns illustrated in the following diagrams can be mapped directly to small variations of the Internet Data Center illustrated in Figure 4.1.

Web-Based User Interface Scenarios

The two deployment scenarios outlined in the following discussion are common variations found when working with Web-based user interfaces.

Web Farm with Local Business Logic

A Web farm with local business logic is a common deployment pattern that places all application components—user interface components (ASP.NET pages), user process components (if used), business components, and data access components—on the Web farm servers. Having the data access on the Web farm allows you to use data readers for fast data rendering. This pattern provides the highest performance, because all component calls are local, and only the databases are accessed remotely, as illustrated in Figure 4.2.

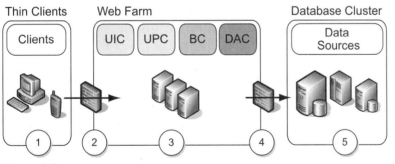

Figure 4.2
Web farm with local business logic

Requirements and considerations for using a Web farm with local business logic include:

- Clients (1) can access the Web farm through a firewall (2) using HTTP and possibly SSL ports.
- The Web farm (3) can host ASP.NET pages and your business components, possibly in Enterprise Services.

- Access to the database is allowed from the Web farm through a firewall (4). The Web farm will need to host client libraries and manage connection strings, which adds important security requirements.
- If the components are using Enterprise Services transactions, RPC ports are open in (4) to allow access to the data sources (5).

Web Farm with Remote Business Logic

Another common deployment pattern is the Web farm with remote business logic. This places all application business components on another farm that is accessed remotely from the ASP.NET pages on the Web farm servers. Performance is slower than in the previous scenario, but this pattern allows multiple clients (for example, desktop clients on an intranet) to share an application farm, which simplifies management. This pattern also provides better separation of the servers managing user interface and the servers managing business transactions, which improves availability by isolating failure points. Scalability may be better in some scenarios where independent resource-intensive operations are needed in both the Web and application farms because these operations will not compete for resources: Your Web servers will serve pages faster and your components will finish sooner.

Figure 4.3 illustrates this deployment pattern.

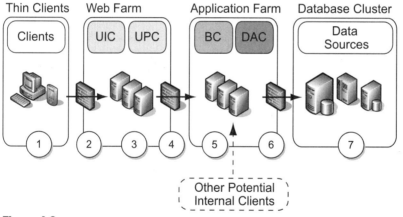

Figure 4.3
Web farm with remote business logic

Requirements and considerations for using a Web farm with remote business logic include:

- Clients (1) can access the Web farm through a firewall (2) using HTTP and possibly SSL ports.
- The Web farm (3) can host ASP.NET pages and user process components. These pages will not be able to take advantage of DataReaders to render data from data

access components unless you deploy data access components on the Web farm and enable the appropriate firewall ports to access the data.

- All business components are hosted in an application farm (5) that other clients can also access. These components are reached through a firewall (4). Depending on the communication channel being used, you may need to open different ports. If your business components are hosted in Enterprise Services, you will need to open RPC ports. For more information about port requirements, see "Designing the Communications Policy" in Chapter 3, "Security, Operational Management, and Communications Policies."

- An infrastructure will typically have either firewall (4) or (6) in place. Internet Data Center provides the capability to have both.

- Access to the database is allowed from the Web farm through the firewall (6). The application farm will need to host client libraries and manage connection strings.

- If the components are using Enterprise Services transactions, RPC ports are open in (6) to allow access to the data sources (7).

Rich Client User Interface Scenarios

The following two scenarios assume a rich client.

Rich Client with Remote Components

A common deployment pattern for rich client applications deployed on an intranet uses remote components. The pattern consists of one server farm that hosts data access components and business components, with all user process and user interface components deployed on the client. as shown in Figure 4.4.

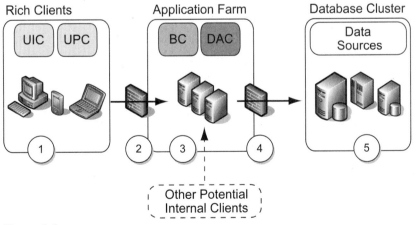

Figure 4.4
Rich client with remote components

Requirements and considerations for using a rich client with remote components include:

- Rich clients (1) have locally deployed user interface components (for example, Windows Forms, user controls, and so on) and user process components (if used). You can deploy these components using SMS, over Active Directory, or download them using HTTP. If your application provides offline functionality, rich clients will also provide the local storage and queuing infrastructure required for offline work.

- Although shown, firewalls (2) and (4) are not present in any but the largest enterprise data centers. Smaller environments will have clients, application servers, and data sources on the intranet with no network separation. Firewall (2) will require ports to be opened for your specific remoting strategy between clients and servers (typically, a TCP port if using .NET remoting, or DCOM ports, and Message Queuing, if used). Firewall (4) will require ports open to access the database and allow for transaction coordination with the data sources.

- Having remote business components in the application farm (3) as shown allows other clients (for example, a Web farm facing the Internet or intranet) share the deployment. Data access components will also be located in this farm and will be accessed remotely from the clients.

Rich Client with Web Service Access

In some cases, you want to provide rich client experience to your users while accessing data and business logic over the Internet. In these cases, you can expose your business logic and data access logic used by the client in a façade or service interface. The rich clients can then invoke this service interface directly with the Web service proxies that Visual Studio .NET generates. Because the rich functionality needed by the user interface is exposed to a larger audience, you must take extra care in the areas of authentication, authorization, and secure communication between clients and the service interface.

Figure 4.5 illustrates the rich client with Web access pattern.

Requirements and considerations for using a rich client with Web service access include:

- This scenario is similar to using a rich client with remote components, except that in this case an XML Web service (ASP.NET .asmx file) service interface provides access to appropriate parts of your application's business logic and data access logic. This service can access your application components locally in the application farm (3) as shown or they can invoke components remotely (not shown).

- Rich clients can access the server functionality using standard protocols and formats. The use of SOAP allows others to build other UI layers that meet their needs.

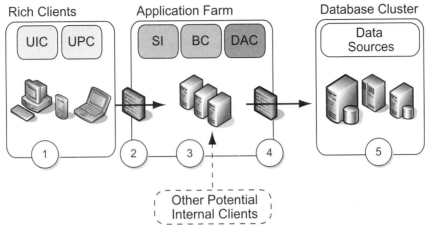

Figure 4.5
Rich client with Web service access

Service Integration Scenarios

The following scenarios show patterns that are commonly used when you need to expose and invoke external services and applications.

Service Agents and Interfaces Deployed with Business Components

Deploying the service interfaces (such as XML Web services) and service agents (components that may call Web Services, or that may connect with other platforms) with the business logic is a scenario very similar to deploying ASP.NET user interfaces and business logic components together. Figure 4.6 on the next page shows a physical deployment pattern for a service-based application.

Requirements and considerations for using service agents and interfaces with local business logic include:

- Clients and services calling into your application (1) can access the Web farm through a firewall (2) using HTTP and possibly SSL ports. The Web farm (3) can host XML Web services, Message Queuing listeners, and other service interface code.

- The service interfaces in the Web farm invoke your business components that will potentially reside in Enterprise Services. When determining the infrastructure for application tiers using Message Queuing, you need to consider the scalability and availability of your application: You will need to make a Web farm to load balance XML Web service calls, but if your components are receiving Message Queuing messages, you will need to build a failover cluster to ensure the message store availability. Because components may be farmed, a failover cluster may not be the most economically efficient way to utilize the servers. You may decide to split the infrastructure pattern used for Message Queuing messages and XML

Web service calls if a small set of computers cannot provide your scalability and availability requirements.

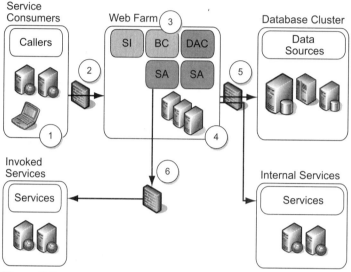

Figure 4.6
A service with local business logic

- Calls to data sources (4) and internal services (5) can be initiated anywhere from the farm. This requires that the firewall at (5) allow outgoing calls (HTTP calls in the case of Web services). In Internet Data Center, outgoing calls to outside services are made through a separate logical firewall (6). Using a different firewall to allow incoming and outgoing HTTP sessions to the Internet can increase security if the computers making the calls and those receiving them are on different VLANs. With the appropriate firewall rules, firewalls (2) and (6) can be merged.

- Access to the data sources is allowed from the Web farm through the firewall at (5). The Web farm will need to host client libraries and manage connection strings, which adds important security requirements.

- If the components are using Enterprise Services transactions, RPC ports are open in (5) to allow access to the data sources. Message Queuing ports may be need to be opened on this firewall if queues are used to communicate with the internal services.

Business Components Separated from Service Agents and Interfaces

Another pattern used in service integration scenarios is the separation of business components from the service agents and service interfaces. This infrastructure model is used to separate the tiers that have contact with the Internet (either by receiving calls or by making calls to other servers) from the farms hosting business logic. When using this pattern, you also need to deploy service agent components in a different cluster when using clustered Message Queuing to receive messages, so that you can achieve availability and still have a load-balanced farm hosting your business components. Figure 4.7 shows this approach.

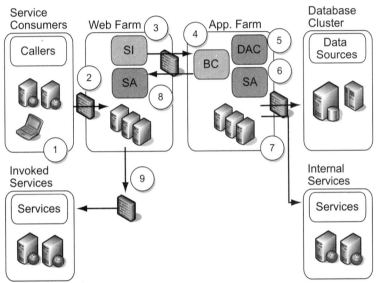

Figure 4.7
Isolating service agents in a separate farm

Requirements and considerations for using a Web farm with remote business logic include:

- Calling services (1) can access the service interfaces in the Web farm (3) hosting XML Web services or Message Queuing HTTP endpoints through a firewall (2) using HTTP and possibly SSL ports.
- The Web farm can host XML Web services and possibly data access logic components as discussed in Chapter 2, "Designing the Components of an Application or Service." You can deploy data access components in this Web farm to take advantage of DataReaders to render data for the results of Web service calls.

If you do so, though, you will have to allow database access through a second firewall (4). If this is a security concern, you will have to access the data provided by data access layer components and business components remotely.

- All business components are hosted in an application farm (4) that other clients may also access. These components are reached from the Web farm through the second firewall. Depending on the communication channel being used, you may need to open different ports. If your business components are hosted in Enterprise Services, you will need RPC ports open for DCOM. For more information about port requirements, see "Designing the Communications Policy" in Chapter 3, "Security, Operational Management, and Communications Policies."

- The business components will call data access components (5) and service agents for internal services locally (6). Databases and internal services are accessed through the firewall at (7).

- An infrastructure will typically have either firewall (4) or (7) in place, depending on whether business components can be inside the DMZ or need extra protection. Internet Data Center provides the capability to have both.

- If the components are using Enterprise Services transactions, RPC ports are open in firewall (7) to allow access to the data sources.

- Service agents (8) that need to make calls out to the Internet can be deployed in the Web farm (or another farm) to isolate the tier that has Internet exposure from the business logic that has access to internal databases and services. Note that there are two firewalls separating the application from the Internet – one for incoming calls (2) and one for outgoing calls (9). If you are implementing security by isolation, you should use this deployment pattern to deploy service agents remotely. If you need to consolidate the servers hosting the service interfaces and service agents, you can also merge these two firewalls into one firewall with both outgoing and incoming ports open.

EAI Clusters and Application Components

You should approach Enterprise Application Integration (EAI) infrastructure components separately from the infrastructure that hosts traditional applications.

However, the EAI cluster will probably host business workflows that use business components to implement steps in the business processes. These components may be hosted locally or remotely from the cluster running the business workflow. You have three options in this case:

- You could host the business components locally on the EAI cluster if the EAI cluster can access the database and if the components will only be used in the context of the business workflows that run in this cluster.

- You could call your business components through .NET remoting, DCOM, or XML Web services and access them on the application or Web farm where they are deployed. This implies that your EAI cluster can make calls to the application farm.

- Finally, you could deploy your business components assemblies on both the EAI cluster and the application or Web farm, with the associated management costs of having the same assembly in more than one location.

Figure 4.8 illustrates one configuration option for EAI clusters, in which you separate the EAI components from the business components.

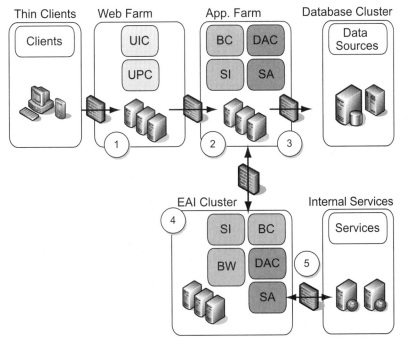

Figure 4.8
Separating EAI components from business components

Figure 4.8 shows user interface components on a Web farm (1) calling business components on an application farm (2), which in turn work with the application data source (3). The EAI cluster (4) has its own business components needed to perform the steps in its business workflows, and accesses other services (in this example, only internal services) through a firewall (5).

Composing Deployment Scenarios

The deployment patterns in the preceding discussions are commonly found in well-architected applications. Of course, particular scenarios may vary, and these examples may not precisely match your requirements and needs. You can compose almost any infrastructure required for a layered application based on these patterns. The important thing is to follow the conceptual model outlined earlier and to understand the application design, the infrastructure design, and how they affect each other early in the application lifecycle.

Production, Test, and Staging Environments

You may have separate data centers for developing, testing, staging, and stress-testing your application. These data centers will usually vary in design, mainly because it is not cost-effective to have a full production data center just for application staging. If your data centers are different, here are some things you should consider:

- **Firewalls**: Even if you don't have firewalls deployed in non-production environments, you should plan ahead and test taking into account port restrictions and direction of communication. Software products that emulate firewalls are available and are a good addition to the test platform.

- **Network topology**: Your staging environment may be smaller than the production environment, but you should strive to keep the network topology consistent. In other words, you want to make sure communication across computers works as expected.

- **Processor count**: If your target environment has multiple processors, you should test your application on multiple processors to make sure multithreaded code will not behave in unexpected ways.

Operational Requirements

The goal of the following discussion is to provide you with design techniques and practices that will enable you to achieve the operational (nonfunctional) requirements for your application and services. These requirements include the levels of scalability, availability, maintainability, security, and manageability your application must achieve. They may affect the design of the application policies, but they will also affect the way you design your application logic.

In some cases, complying with some operational requirements will create challenges to comply with others. For example, it is common to lower the manageability of an application favoring security. It is important to prioritize application features supporting operational requirements early in the life cycle so these tradeoffs and decisions can be factored into the application implementation from the start.

The following discussion is by no means complete, but will help you isolate key issues pertaining important operational requirements.

Scalability

An application's scalability is its ability to provide an acceptable level of overall performance when one or more load factors is increased. Common load factors include the number of users, the amount of data being managed by the application, and the number of transactions.

Overall performance can be measured in terms of throughput and response time. Throughput measures the amount of work that the application can perform in a given time frame, and response time measures the amount of time between a user or a process making a request and seeing the results of the request. A number of factors can affect both throughput and response time, including hardware performance, physical resources such as memory, network latency (the amount of time it takes to transmit data over a network link), and application design. While many performance and scalability issues can be resolved by increasing hardware resources, an application that is not designed to operate efficiently will nearly always perform poorly regardless of how much hardware you throw at the problem.

Consider the following design guidelines for highly scalable applications:

- **Use asynchronous operations**. Reduce response time and throughput demand by using asynchronous operations.

  Synchronous operations require that the user wait until a business operation is complete. By making business operations asynchronous, system control can be returned to the user more quickly and processing requests can be queued, helping to control throughput demand without overwhelming the business components. For example, suppose that a user places an order in an e-commerce site. If the order process is performed synchronously, the user will have to wait until the credit card has been authorized and the goods have been ordered from the supplier before receiving confirmation. If you implement the order process asynchronously, the user can be given a confirmation or failure message by e-mail after the operation is complete. Designing asynchronous applications creates more work for the developer (especially when they require transactional logic) but can greatly improve scalability.

- **Cache data where it is required**. Whenever possible, you should try to cache data at the location where it is required, and therefore minimize the number of remote data requests made to your data store. For example, the e-commerce site described earlier will provide a much higher level of scalability if the product data is cached in the Web site instead of being retrieved from the database each time a user tries to view a list of products.

- **Avoid holding state unnecessarily**. Where possible, you should design your operations to be stateless. Doing so prevents resource contention, improves data consistency, and allows requests to be load balanced across multiple servers in a farm. On some occasions, state will need to be persisted; for example, a customer's shopping cart must be stored across HTTP requests. In these scenarios, you must plan your state persistence and rehydration logic carefully. You should only rehydrate state when it is actually needed (for example, when a user wants to view their shopping cart or check out).

- **Avoid resource contention**. Some resources, such as database connections, are limited, and some resources, such as database locks, are exclusive. You should design your application in such a way that resources are held for the shortest possible time. You should use database connection pooling effectively, and you should design operations to open the most contentious resources last (so that they are not held for the entire operation). This is particularly true when using atomic transactions. For example, if the **Orders** table of a database is used by many parts of the application, you should make the insertion of order data the last step in the ordering process to avoid holding a lock on the table while waiting for credit card authorization.

- **Partition data, resources, and operations**. You can spread the load of your application across farms of servers using load balancing technologies such as Network Load Balancing. This allows you to adopt a "scale out" strategy whereby you increase scalability simply by adding more servers to the farm. Scaling out is usually more cost effective than scaling up by adding hardware resources to your servers.

  Databases should be scaled up primarily by adding hardware resources, but you can also scale out data by partitioning your database across multiple database servers, with each server assuming responsibility for a subset of the data. Dynamic data routing logic is used in the middle-tier to direct requests to the appropriate database server. For more information about partitioning a SQL Server database, see Chapter 5, "SQL Server Database Design" in the "Internet Data Center Reference Architecture Guide" on MSDN (*http://www.microsoft.com /technet/treeview/default.asp?url=/technet/itsolutions/idc/rag/ragc05.asp*).

Availability

Availability is a measure of the percentage of time your application is able to respond to requests in a way that its callers expect. It is generally accepted that even the most robust of applications must occasionally be unavailable, but you should design your application in such a way that the risk of unexpected outages is minimized. For business critical applications, many organizations aim for "five nines," or 99.999% availability, and this level of robustness requires careful planning and design.

Consider the following high availability strategies for application design:

- **Avoid single points of failure**. In your application design and deployment infrastructure, you should try to avoid having any single component that, if taken offline, would render the application unusable. You can avoid single points of failure in a Web or application farm by using load balancing management software, such as that provided with Microsoft Application Center, which will remove an unresponsive server from a load balanced farm without disrupting the operations of the remaining servers.

  You should store business data in data stores (such as databases or queues) that are deployed in failover clusters, so that if a server controlling the data store fails for any reason, the application will "fail over" to the standby server. You should also provide redundant data paths so that there is more than one physical network path to the database server, allowing the application to continue to function in the event of a network cable failure.

  To protect the application from hard disk failures, disk redundancy measures such as Redundant Array of Inexpensive Disk (RAID) technologies should be used.

- **Use caching and queuing to minimize "same time and place" requirements**. Caching read-only reference data where it is needed not only provides improved scalability, but it also reduces reliance on the underlying data store. In the event that the database becomes unavailable, the application can continue to function because the data is still available in the cache.

  Similarly, by queuing requests to insert or update data, the application can still service client requests even when the underlying data sources and services are unavailable. This would allow an e-commerce organization to continue taking orders, even though the order data could not be written to the database immediately.

- **Plan an effective backup strategy**. Regardless of the high availability measures in place, you must ensure that you have an effective backup strategy that minimizes the time taken to recover the system to an operable state in the event of a catastrophic failure.

- **Rigorously test and debug your code**. Of course, you should always test and debug your code, but when high availability is a requirement it is even more important to ensure that you remove any potential infinite loops, memory leaks, or unhandled exceptions that might cause the application to fail or stop responding.

Maintainability

With respect to maintainability, your application should be designed and deployed in such a way that it can be maintained and repaired easily.

Consider the following recommendations for designing a maintainable application:

- **Structure your code in a predictable manner**. Keeping your coding techniques consistent throughout the application makes it easier to maintain. You should use a standardized convention for namespace, variable, class, and constant names, consistent array boundaries, and inline comments.

- **Isolate frequently changing data and behavior**. Encapsulate frequently changing logic and data into separate components that can be updated independent of the rest of the application.

- **Use metadata for configuration and program parameters**. Storing application configuration data, such as connection strings and environmental variables, in external metadata repositories, such as XML configuration files, makes it easy to change these values in the production environment without editing code or recompiling the application. For more information about using metadata, see "Designing the Operational Management Policy" in Chapter 3, "Security, Operational Management, and Communications Policies."

- **Use pluggable types**. When a certain piece of application logic can be implemented in many ways, it is useful to define an interface and have the application load the correct class that implements the interface at run time. This lets you "plug in" other components that implement the interface after the application has been deployed without having to modify it. You can store fully qualified type names in a configuration store and use them to instantiate objects at run time. When using this approach, you must ensure that your configuration store is adequately secured to prevent an attacker from forcing your application to use a component of his or her own devising.

- **Interface design**. Design your component interfaces so that all public properties and method parameters are of common types. Using common types reduces dependencies between your component and its consumers.

Security

Security is always a major concern when designing an application, particularly when the application will be exposed to the Web. To a large extent, the decisions you make regarding security will depend on your security policy. Regardless of the specific details of your security policy, you should always consider the following recommendations:

- **Evaluate the risks**. Take some time during the design of your application to evaluate the risks posed by each implementation or deployment decision. Remember to consider internal risks, as well as those posed by external hackers.

For example, you may use secure HTTP connections to prevent a customer's credit card number from being "sniffed" as it is passed to your site over the Internet, but if you then store the credit card number in plain text in your database, you run the risk of an unauthorized employee obtaining it.

- **Apply the principle of "least privilege."** The principle of least privilege is a standard security design policy that ensures each user account has exactly the right level of privilege to perform the tasks required of it *and no more*. For example, if an application needs to read data from a file, the user account it uses should be assigned **Read** permission, not **Modify**, or **Full Control**. No account should have permission to do anything it does not need to do.

- **Perform authentication checks at the boundary of each security zone.** Authentication should always be performed "at the gate." A user's process should not be allowed to perform any tasks in a given security zone until a valid identity has been established.

- **Carefully consider the role of user context in asynchronous business processes.** When your application performs business tasks asynchronously, remember that user context is less meaningful than if the task is performed synchronously. You should consider using a "trusted server" model for asynchronous operations, rather than an impersonation/delegation approach.

Manageability

Your organization's operational management policy will determine the aspects of your application that need to be managed. You should design instrumentation into your application so that it exposes the critical management information needed for health monitoring, service level agreement (SLA) verification, and capacity planning. For a more complete discussion about management of distributed .NET-based applications, see Chapter 3, "Security, Operational Management, and Communications Policies."

Performance

Application and service performance is critical to a good user experience and efficient hardware utilization. While performance is an attribute that can be improved by tuning the implementation and code of the system after it is built, it is important to give thought to performance at the architecture and design stages. While a detailed discussion on profiling is beyond the scope of this guide, you may want to follow this process at various stages in application prototyping, development, testing, and so on to make sure that performance goals are met, or that expectations are being reset as early as possible:

1. Define the measurable performance requirements for specific operations (for example, throughput and/or latency under certain utilization, such as "50 requests per second with 70% average CPU usage on a specific hardware configuration").

2. Do performance testing: Stress test the system and collect profiling information.

3. Analyze the test results: Does the application meet the performance goals?

4. If the application does not meet the performance goals, identify bottlenecks in the application. (For tools that can help you isolate performance bottlenecks, see the articles referred to at the end of this list.)

5. Repeat Step 2 until the performance results meet the goals.

The following articles contain information needed to perform this process:

".NET Framework SDK: Enabling Profiling" (*http://msdn.microsoft.com/library /default.asp?url=/library/en-us/cpguide/html/cpconenablingprofiling.asp?frame=true*)

".NET CLR Profiling Services: Track Your Managed Components to Boost Application Performance," MSDN Magazine, November 2001 (*http://msdn.microsoft.com /msdnmag/issues/01/11/NetProf/NetProf.asp*)

Appendixes

This section includes the following appendixes:

- Appendix 1: Layered Architectures

  This appendix explains the relationship between the layers described in this guide and other naming schemes commonly used in the computer industry.

- Appendix 2: Glossary

  This appendix provides a glossary of technical terms relating to distributed application development.

Appendix 1: Layered Architectures

This guide has split an application into layers with distinct roles and functionalities with the goal of helping you maximize the maintainability of the code, optimize the way the application works when deployed in different ways, and provide a clear location where certain technology or design decisions must be made when building distributed applications based on the .NET Framework.

Splitting application functionality into layers has been done by the design pattern community. This table is intended to roughly illustrate how the component layers that are described in this guide map to the terminology for layers and design patterns used by some of these authors.

This guide	Related patterns and layers
User Interface Components	Presentation Layer View Layer Client Layer
User Interface Processes	Application Controller Pattern Controller/Mediator Layer Application Model Layer
Service Interfaces	Remote Façade Pattern
Business Workflows	Domain Layer[2]
Business Components	Domain Layer Transaction Script Pattern
Business Entities	Data Transfer Object[1] Domain Model
Data Access Logic Components[3]	Data Source Layer Infrastructure Layer Integration Layer
Service Agents[3]	Data Source Layer Infrastructure Layer Integration Layer

Notes on the table:

1. Using the data transfer object design pattern for business entity components assumes you are using the business entities as the way you transfer data between layers, either by using ADO.NET DataSets or your custom serializable objects. Another use for business entities that goes beyond the data transfer object pattern is to build an object model or domain model for the whole application, encapsulating both business behavior and state.

2. Business workflows can be thought of as a set of transaction script patterns that has the capability to track and persist state across incoming calls from asynchronous and synchronous callers. It is grouped under domain here because business workflows in the end implement business logic.

3. Data access logic components and service agents may be used to encapsulate data mapping and aggregation/de-aggregation activities, in which case they can be referred to as a data mapping layer or data mapper, depending on the author.

Appendix 2: Glossary

Assembly

An assembly is a unit of deployment in an application based on the .NET framework.

Atomic Transaction

An atomic transaction is an operation in which either all steps in the operation succeed, or they all fail. Atomic transactions are commonly used to perform data modifications in a data store, where either all the data relating to the operation is successfully modified, or none of it is modified and the data remains as it was before the operation started.

Commutativity

Commutativity is a design pattern for an implementation in which *messages* will result in the same outcome, regardless of the order they are received in. For example, a commutative operation might involve two steps: "change product two's category to 'widget'" and "increase product two's price by 10%." It doesn't matter in what order these steps are performed; the net result is that product two is in the "widget" category and has had its price increased by 10%. Conversely, an operation in which the two steps are "change product two's category to 'widget'" and "increase the price of all widgets by 10%" is not commutative, because product two's price will be increased only if its category is changed before the price increase step is performed.

Component

In simple terms, a component is a part of an overall system. A more specific definition of component is a unit of functionality that can be amortized across multiple implementations. A component is usually implemented as a software object that exposes one or more interfaces and that implements logic.

Contract

A contract is a binding agreement between multiple parties that dictates the valid communication semantics. The contract determines the protocols used to communicate and the format of *messages* as well as the service level agreement and legal declarations.

Conversation

A conversation is the exchange of messages between a client application and a *service* that is required to complete a business task.

CRUD

CRUD is an abbreviation of Create, Read, Update, and Delete. It refers to the operations that can be performed in a data store. In SQL terms, Create, Read, Update, and Delete refer to INSERT, SELECT, UPDATE, and DELETE operations respectively.

Demilitarized Zone (DMZ)

A DMZ is the physical *zone* behind an Internet facing *firewall* and in front of a second level firewall that protects back-end systems and data. In a typical Internet application scenario, the DMZ is the physical virtual local area network (VLAN) on which the Web servers are deployed.

Dynamic Data Routing

Dynamic data routing is logic that is used to determine which database server to send a date retrieval or modification request to when the data is partitioned across multiple servers. DDR can be implemented using a hashing algorithm, a rule table, or some other partitioning scheme.

Emissary

An emissary is a generic term for a software component that communicates with an external resource on behalf of your application. The emissary abstracts the semantics of communicating with the external resource from your application, and it manages all aspects of the *conversation*, including the persistence of state for long-running processes.

Fiefdom

A fiefdom is a design pattern for a collection of services that encapsulate shared durable state and are deployed together. A fiefdom represents a boundary of trust, where the software components inside the fiefdom distrust those outside.

Firewall

A firewall is a software- or hardware-based security implementation that applies filtering rules to network traffic between two zones.

Idempotency

Idempotency means the ability to perform a particular action multiple times and still achieve the same result as you would when performing it once. An idempotent message such as an instruction to "change the price of product two to $10.00" will cause no side effect when received multiple times, whereas a non-idempotent message such as an instruction to "increase the price of product two by 10%" will produce a different result depending on how many times it is received.

Layer

A layer can be thought of as an architecture pattern in which components use services in layers below. Layering helps maintainability. The communication between two layers determines how well the application can be partitioned at that point for physical distribution across tiers. Strict layering schemes don't allow layers to access anything but the layers immediately below, while relaxed layering schemes allow a given layer to use any other layer below it.

Long-Running Transaction

A long-running transaction is an implementation of a business process or part of a business process that contains the logic to compensate for the activities that have already been executed in case of cancellation.

Message

A message is a unit of information transmitted electronically from one service to another.

Orchestration

Orchestration is the automation of a *workflow*. Microsoft BizTalk® Server provides an orchestration engine that can be used to orchestrate business workflows.

Policy

A policy is a set of rules with respect to security, operational management, and communication that is applicable in a specific *zone*.

Service

A service is a software component that can be used in part of an overall business process. Services support a message-based communication interface, through which a *conversation* takes place. A service encapsulates its own state and business data, and it can be communicated with only through the *service interfaces* it exposes.

Service Agent

A service agent is an *emissary* that is used to handle a *conversation* with an external service.

Service Interface

A service interface is an entry point for a service. It provides a public interface that callers can use to query the *contract* supported through the interface and make message-based method calls to the service.

Stateful

Stateful is the opposite of stateless. In a stateful *conversation*, information relating to aspects of previously exchanged data must be recorded to allow meaningful exchanges subsequently.

Stateless

Stateless refers to a *conversation* in which all messages between parties can be interpreted independently. No state is held between messages.

Two-Phase Commit

The two-phase commit protocol is used to ensure that multiple parties synchronize their state when a transactional operation is performed. The two-phase commit protocol can be used for atomic transactions as well as for business transactions.

Workflow

Workflow refers to a business process in which steps must be performed in a particular order, and predefined conditions must be met, before moving from one step to the next. For example, a workflow for purchasing goods might involve first validating the purchaser's credit card details, then ordering the goods from a supplier, and finally arranging delivery. The goods cannot be ordered until the credit card details are authorized, and delivery cannot be arranged until the goods have been received from the supplier.

Zone

A zone is a trust boundary, a communication boundary, and an operational boundary. The zone may map to a real-world entity, such as a company or department, or it may define a particular area within the physical deployment environment of the application, such as a Web farm or even just a process. Zones are useful mental models when determining application deployment and the relationship of application design to the infrastructure design.

Feedback and Support

Questions? Comments? Suggestions? To give feedback on this guide, please send an e-mail message to devfdbck@microsoft.com.

Collaborators and Contributors

Solution Architect & Program Manager: Edward A. Jezierski

Many thanks to our collaborators, sponsors and reviewers:

Keith Short, Mike Pizzo, Johannes Klein, Rodney Limprecht, Chris Anderson, Anders Hejlsberg, Mark Anders, David Treadwell, Jonathan Hawkins, Erik Olson, Brad Rhodes, Rob Howard, Ron Jacobs, John Shewchuck, Luca Bolognese, David Schleifer, Riyaz Pishori, Pablo Castro, Brian Pepin, Mark Boulter, Shawn Burke, Michael Platt, Maarten Mullender, Mike Burner, Dino Chiesa, John Montgomery, Richard Burte, Steve Kirk, Richard Irving, Srinath Vasireddy, Steve Newbury, Sharon Bjeltich, Tom Devey, Kurt Schenk, Bryan Lamos, Paddy Srinivasan, Yves Dolce, Rob Macdonald, Mark Phillips, Blair Shaw, Jeremy Rule, Paul Gomes, Dale Michalk, Martin Petersen-Frey, Angela Crocker, Kenny Jones, Ilia Fortunov, Shantanu Sarkar, Rossen Blagoev, the Think Tank, Bijan Javidi, Bob Jarvis, Aaron Margosis, Maurice Magnier, Doug Orange, Eugenio Pace, Carlos Billy Reynoso, Anthony Menio, Karl Schulmeisters, Ingo Ramner, Bernard Chen (Sapient), Dimitris Georgakopoulos (Sapient), Michael Monteiro (Sapient), Roger Sessions (ObjectWatch), Andrew Roubin, Diego Gonzalez (Lagash), Adrie Geelhoed (CMG), Gerke Geurts (CMG), Sasha Siddhartha, and Franco Ceruti (VBNext).

Prescriptive Architecture Guidance and content team:

Technical Writers: Graeme Malcolm (Content Master Ltd) and Lin Joyner (Content Master Ltd)

Technical Editor: Tina Burden (Entirenet)

Filiberto Selvas Patiño, Michael Kropp, Per Vonge Nielsen, Shaun Hayes, J.D. Meier, Rick Maguire, Philip Teale, Ken Perilman, David Trowbridge, Mohammad Al-Sabt, Lars Laakes, Sharon Smith, Chris Sfanos, Claudia Iebbiano (Wadeware) and the architecture review board from Satyam Computer Services Ltd.

Microsoft®

patterns & practices

Proven practices for predictable results

Patterns & practices are Microsoft's recommendations for architects, software developers, and IT professionals responsible for delivering and managing enterprise systems on the Microsoft platform. Patterns & practices are available for both IT infrastructure and software development topics.

Patterns & practices are based on real-world experiences that go far beyond white papers to help enterprise IT pros and developers quickly deliver sound solutions. This technical guidance is reviewed and approved by Microsoft engineering teams, consultants, Product Support Services, and by partners and customers. Organizations around the world have used patterns & practices to:

Reduce project cost

- Exploit Microsoft's engineering efforts to save time and money on projects
- Follow Microsoft's recommendations to lower project risks and achieve predictable outcomes

Increase confidence in solutions

- Build solutions on Microsoft's proven recommendations for total confidence and predictable results
- Provide guidance that is thoroughly tested and supported by PSS, not just samples, but production quality recommendations and code

Deliver strategic IT advantage

- Gain practical advice for solving business and IT problems today, while preparing companies to take full advantage of future Microsoft technologies.

To learn more about *patterns & practices* visit: *msdn.microsoft.com/practices*

To purchase *patterns & practices* guides visit: *shop.microsoft.com/practices*

patterns & practices
Proven practices for predictable results

patterns & practices

Proven practices for predictable results

Patterns & practices are available for both IT infrastructure and software development topics. There are four types of patterns & practices available:

Reference Architectures

Reference Architectures are IT system-level architectures that address the business requirements, operational requirements, and technical constraints for commonly occurring scenarios. Reference Architectures focus on planning the architecture of IT systems and are most useful for architects.

Reference Building Blocks

References Building Blocks are re-usable sub-systems designs that address common technical challenges across a wide range of scenarios. Many include tested reference implementations to accelerate development.

Reference Building Blocks focus on the design and implementation of sub-systems and are most useful for designers and implementors.

Operational Practices

Operational Practices provide guidance for deploying and managing solutions in a production environment and are based on the Microsoft Operations Framework. Operational Practices focus on critical tasks and procedures and are most useful for production support personnel.

Patterns

Patterns are documented proven practices that enable re-use of experience gained from solving similar problems in the past. Patterns are useful to anyone responsible for determining the approach to architecture, design, implementation, or operations problems.

To learn more about *patterns & practices* visit: *msdn.microsoft.com/practices*

To purchase *patterns & practices* guides visit: *shop.microsoft.com/practices*

patterns & practices current titles

For current list of titles visit: *msdn.microsoft.com/practices*

To purchase *patterns & practices* guides visit: *shop.microsoft.com/practices*

patterns & practices

Proven practices for predictable results